GOT A QUESTION?

Life gives you a lot
to think about . . .

Interactive readings for you & others

Pastor Chris Brekke

Got a Question?

Copyright © 2018 by Chris Brekke

ISBN: 978-0-9981476-4-2

Illustrations © Chris Brekke

Format/Design by Minion Editing & Design
www.joyminion.com

Published by J.O.Y. Publishing
Printed in the United States of America

*To order extra copies of this book,
please contact Pastor Brekke:*

Phone: **651.600.9964**
Email: **Cjbrekke51@gmail.com**
Mail: **2700 Oxvord Street N #136
Roseville, MN 55113**

Or order from Sola Publishing:
www.solapublishing.com

CONTENTS

Preface

Life Questions 1

1. Do Nice People Get Worn Out? 2
2. Is Life Just Painful and Pointless? 4
3. How Do You Know Whose Message is True? 6
4. Can People Not Be So Divided? 8
5. Why Does Our Faith Have So Many Rules? 10
6. What If the Truth Hurts? 12
7. When Should We Be Not So Nice? 14
8. What If I Just Can't Forgive? 16
9. Do You Ever Just Want to Die? 18
10. What Are You Trying to Achieve? 20
11. Do We Humans Run the World? 22
12. Do You Want Justice? 24
13. Are My Days Numbered? 26
14. Will We Humans Ever Wise Up? 28
15. What Do You Think of Parental Authority? 30
16. Are We More Than Physical? 32
17. Is It OK to Relax? 34
18. How Many Loaves Do You Have? 36
19. Is Prosperity a Test? 38
20. Isn't the World Dreadful? 40
21. Does Good Behavior Pay? 42
22. What Are You Afraid Of? 44
23. Is the Flat-Earth Society Growing? 46
24. Are People Stupid? 48
25. Do you Have Enemies? 50
26. Are Your Children Yours? 52
27. Can We Be Spiritual But Not Religious? 54
28. What's Your Dream? 56

God Questions 59
29. What Sort of God Do We Have? 60
30. Isn't God a Loser at Love? 62
31. Isn't Leviticus Obsolete? 64
32. Does God Hide From Us? 66
33. Is God Really With Us? 68
34. How is it That God Cares for Us? 70
35. Why is the Bible Critical of Us? 72
36. If We Know Him, Will We Love Him? 74
37. Why Should I Be Thankful? 76
38. Was Jesus a Spelunker? 78
39. Where Can a Person Find God? 80
40. Why is Christmas Such a Big Deal? 82
41. How Does God Call Someone? 84
42. What is the "Kingdom of God"? 86
43. Is God Usually Incognito? 88
44. Who's Got the Holy Spirit? 90
45. What's With the Trinity-Thing? 92
46. Does God Pick Sides? 94
47. Does God Spank? 96
48. Does God Get Thwarted? 98
49. Do You Need a Sign From God? 100
50. Does God End People's Lives? 102
51. Does Satan Attack People? 104
52. Does God Dither? 106

Faith Questions 109
   53. Why Doesn't Christianity Work Better? 110
   54. Why Don't I Feel Like Worshiping? 112
   55. Can God's Enemies Become Allies? 114
   56. Is Heartfelt Faith Kinda Embarrassing? 116
   57. Can I Be a Christian Without a Church? 118
   58. Can Our Faith Be Stolen? 120
   59. Were Those Bible Heroes Almost Perfect? 122
   60. Who Kisses in Church? 124
   61. Must Christians Submit? 126
   62. Want Some Advice for Being a Christian? 128
   63. What Do People Pray About? 130
   64. Are Christians Strange? 132
   65. Does it Matter How I Dress? 134
   66. Is Christianity a Caucasian Thing? 136
   67. What Happens in Baptism? 138
   68. How Adaptable Can We Be? 140
   69. Are Christians Crackpots? 142
   70. Should Christians be Activists? 144
   71. Is Communion Cannibalism? 146
   72. Is Christianity Exclusive? 148
   73. Do I Have to Tell Others About Jesus? 150
   74. Are You Ready for the Worst? 152
   75. Is Christianity Conservative or Liberal? 154
   76. Is It OK to Be Rich? 156
   77. Are Christians Better Than Non-Christians? ... 158
   78. Must I Choose Between Secular Values and Christian Values? 160
   79. Who Should I Give To? 162
   80. Should We Praise God in Our Troubles? 164

Topical Index 166
About the Author 168

PREFACE

"GOT A QUESTION?"

Got a Question? Probably so. We humans are blessed with inquisitive minds. We want to know things. If you have questions about God or life or faith, this little book aims to offer encouragement and inspiration to you. Just thumb through and find one that grabs you.

Jesus frequently used questions in His encounters with people. Questions got them thinking, and opened new pathways for discovery. The Master Teacher used that method; so now some of His apprentices try it too.

✛✛ If you want to double the benefit of this book, use it in a group. Be it with your family or some friends or your youth group, try this:

1. Read the Question

2. Have people share their thoughts on it

3. Read the devotion

4. Discuss more

5. Pray together about the topic

Thus . . . INTERACTIVE DEVOTIONS.

The "answers" to the questions are fairly brief here. They are perhaps just crumbs, when there is no doubt a whole loaf/book dealing with each matter. I hope the "crumbs" will help a little, and also stimulate your appetite for more of the truth that stands the test of time. (Gifted theologians write volumes; others of us offer crumbs.)

A pen is not provided, but please feel free to be interactive with this book: jot reactions, ideas, and your own questions in the margins. Doodle even, as some say that doodling is a catalyst for creative thinking.

On each page, one word is *underlined*. This keyword can be used to prompt discussion or study on that topic. Plus, there is a topical index in the back, with related Bible verses on the topic.

LIFE QUESTIONS

How does the world work & what sort of creatures are we?

Wisdom

1
DO NICE PEOPLE GET WORN OUT?

"But Elijah went a day's journey into the wilderness, and came and sat down under a broom tree; and he asked that he might die, saying 'it is enough; now, O Lord, take away my life; for I am no better than my fathers.'" — 1 Kings 19:4

You probably don't need to be told that life can sock it to you. There are times when you've just had it. "Enough is enough." This happens not only to the unspiritual, but to strong believers as well. All of us are vulnerable to weariness and despondency. One of the Bible's superstars, Elijah, experienced such a collapse. Not long after his greatest spiritual victory, over the prophets of Baal on Mt Carmel, Elijah found himself on the run for his life. Wicked Queen Jezebel had pledged to hunt Elijah down and kill him. (Read all about it in 1 Kings 19.) Even this mighty man of God was ready to call it quits. He was down and out and fully <u>discouraged</u> and wanted to just die. It appeared that all his work had been in vain. He felt utterly alone and hopeless. You sure don't want this happening to you, nor to those you love! Alas, it might. The world can be so difficult and draining. So, if it happens, then what?

The Lord does not give Elijah a terse "buck up"..."quit pouting"..."move on." God does not offer him a tidy Bible verse or a pious platitude. He lets Elijah have some space, lets him sleep, and feeds him. God grants recovery time. He refills Elijah's cup. They talk. God came to him not in a mighty show of force, but in a "*still small voice.*" The Lord who specializes in redemption of the down and out does not give up on the overburdened and frail prophet. You see the tender nourishment that Elijah needed, and got; and you know others who today need such TLC. God is good. God is patient. God is able to rebuild and reuse those who have fallen. Ah, the wonderful love of the Lord.

Notice also that God sent reinforcements. He did not leave Elijah to go it alone. The weight of the world and the battle against evil was not all on him. The Lord would call Elisha now to step in. This is critical. Do not let others fight alone on the battlefield. How wise and good of our God to provide allies! Together we rise to do His will. Though the struggle be long, the Lord is strong.

Notes

2
IS LIFE JUST PAINFUL AND POINTLESS?

"I have seen everything that is done under the sun; and behold, all is vanity and a striving after the wind." — Ecclesiastes 1:14

Never read Ecclesiastes when you are feeling blue. It is grim and hopeless and would turn you a deeper shade of blue. It has such a dire view of life that one might wonder why it is in the Good Book. It is far from uplifting. Here's the setup: old King Solomon has turned sour about life. You may remember that this is the guy who was ultra-wise and mega-rich. He lived in a palace with many, many wives and great power. The wealth and admiration of the nations flowed to him. He wrote the book of Proverbs, which is upbeat wisdom literature — a sunny prosperity manual on how to make it successfully in the world. It is fun and smart, and is followed immediately in the Bible by Ecclesiastes. Talk about a 180° turn! These books go directly from rosy optimism to dreary <u>doubt</u>. Solomon's repeated thought becomes, "*Vanity, vanity, all is vanity.*" Some newer translations use the word "*pointless.*" His worldview now is "first you suffer, then you die."

So what happened? Old age? Perhaps that's part of it. Solomon still had his wealth and power, but that wasn't enough. His kingdom has become splintered, his body has begun the downturn, and his future is as worm food. He is smart enough to know it. Rather than mindlessly carry on, pretending all will be well (as many humans try to do), Solomon faces the grim truth: life has a hopeless end. Human glory ends in tragedy. No one gets out alive. It's the death march to oblivion. It's pointless. Solomon is sadly correct. Unless...

There is a Savior. Poor Solomon did not have what we have. He did not know, 1,000 years before the coming of Jesus, that God could and would bail us out. Solomon had been spiritually corrupted by his many foreign wives — he had become polytheistic (a modern now would call him "multi-culturally diverse") — and he had no devotion to the Lord. He had no intimacy with the One who is eternal, so he ended up honestly and depressingly mortal. And that is why Ecclesiastes is in the Scripture. It pulls no punches. It tells us the bitter truth: without the Lord to rescue us, there is no hope. We in Christ get the sweet, sweet news: instead of a hopeless end, we have an endless hope!

Notes

3
How Do You Know Whose Message Is True?

"Behold, I am against the prophets, 'says the Lord, who use their tongues and say 'Says the Lord.'"
— Jeremiah 23:31

Sometimes a True/False question is easy. Sometimes it is not. Your odds are 50/50 at least. Getting the true and false correct can be so vital, though often difficult. A small town I lived in had a saying: "Half of what you hear on the streets is true. The problem is in figuring out which half." The town gossip mill was busy. Busy too are the message-mills of our country. Lots of voices and viewpoints are available. And which are true? Who is spinning the truth and who is telling the truth? Who do you believe?

Way back in Bible-days they also struggled with matters of <u>truth</u> and falsehood. The prophet Jeremiah had slews of countervailing voices speaking in opposition to him. They too claimed to speak for God. Jeremiah was speaking a hard truth: "Shape up and change your ways or the Lord is gonna bring down the hammer." The other prophets said: "No, no, don't panic and listen to that crackpot Jeremiah. He's just a gloom-and-doom negative ninny." So which message would the people listen to? Which message was true and which was false?

If you do a Bible search on false prophets, you'd find that there were many, and that often the people were led astray, and that one didn't really know for sure until things played out. That's not very encouraging, is it? How do we then tell God's true voice among the plethora of sounds we hear purporting to give us the true Word? As you may know, there are tens of thousands of Christian denominations, each one claiming to speak for God. Many folks in our 21st century now seem to be "post-modern" about this — meaning that they see truth as subjective and malleable. You've heard someone say, "That may be true for you but it is not true for me." Oh, boy — that leaves you stranded.

Christians have some truth-tests:

1. Does it line up with God's eternal Word of Scripture?
2. Does it bear good fruit?
3. Is it consistent with the wisdom and counsel of God's Church over the ages?
4. Does it point people to Him who is the Way the Truth and the Life?

Seek the leading of the Lord, with others. His truth shall prevail.

Notes

4
CAN PEOPLE NOT BE SO DIVIDED?

"For I know their works and their thoughts, and I am coming to gather all nations and tongues; and they shall come and shall see my glory."
— Isaiah 66:18

What an immense variety of peoples and tribes are on the earth. How many countries can you name? How many languages? How many identity groupings even within our own country? And how are we doing with that? Do racial groups refrain from associating with other racial groups? I'm afraid they do. Do the urban "elites" think themselves superior to the rural folks? Probably. Do folks from the East Coast and the Left Coast call the Midwest "fly-over country"? Yes, they do. Do we keep distance from those who are not like us? I'd guess so. Sad to say: our tribalism is innate, and strong. God has His work cut out for Him. If we are to affirm people of different classes and cultures and colors, it will take a miracle. Good thing we serve a Lord who does miracles!

This is nothing new. Way back in Bible days, prophets like Isaiah could see that God had a much larger vision for His Kingdom than the Israelites did. They, like most all groups, wanted to draw a line around their own. They thought that God was theirs to be blessed by. They needed their loving room enlarged. Isaiah said that God's reign would include people in "*Tarshish, Put, and Lud*" (where?).... And even "*the distant coastlands.*" This was not in the promised land. These foreigners were not from Abraham, Isaac and Jacob. They "*had not heard of God's name nor seen His glory.*" Yet Isaiah foretold that "*they would come,*" and "*all people will come to worship me.*" This massive expansion of the Lord's domain is a mark of His glory. He desires _unity_ for all His children.

So the Father loves the whole world; not just some. Rich and poor, young and old, black and white, rural and urban, conservative and liberal — all are invited in. God loves all. Can we? What a test of life the Lord gives us. Will we love only our own, or will we expand the borders of our goodwill? Our Christ created His Church in part for just this purpose. He wants a people whose welcome is wide. He's got a big, big house!

Notes

5
WHY DOES OUR FAITH HAVE SO MANY RULES?

"Do not neglect to show hospitality to strangers.... Remember those who are in prison....Let marriage be held in honor....Keep your life free from the love of money." — Hebrews 13:2-5

Our 66-book Bible is a potpourri of literature types. The Good Book is not all one thing. It's got history, and poetry, and instructions, and prayers, and prophecy, and of course the proclamation of life's greatest news. Think with me about those instructions. Be it commandments or parables or proverbs, be it from Moses or Jesus or Solomon, much of the Bible exists to teach us how to live as the people of the Lord. There's no denying that we need the help, eh? We are flawed fools who regularly make a royal mess of things. So God in His goodness has advice for us. For our best interests, He says, *"Do this and live"* and *"follow these instructions and you will be blessed."* Thank God for His guidance!

We Christians know that such *instructions* and our keeping of them do not save us. We just are not good enough nor smart enough for that to work. We are saved only by the sheer and drastic grace of God poured out in

$-10-$

Jesus. Our sole hope is in Him, not in our success on the performance plan of following instructions. So we are not saved by faithful obedience to what the Lord commands, but we are saved for faithful obedience to those commands. God has lots of good for us to do, and lots of blessings to impart. Those who are saved want to glorify the Lord by living as He wants. We know that His rules are life-giving.

Then these instructions are well-received and gladly pursued. In Hebrews 13, for example, we Christ-followers are instructed on many topics. They include: hospitality, visitation, marriage, money, leaders and worship. All of these are involved in discipleship, as we seek to learn how to serve Christ in every area of life. I bet you can do some self-inventory on a topic or two from this list, and let God teach you a thing or two. That would be beneficial — for you, and also for those around you. As we grow in our imitation of Jesus, we display marks of discipleship that honor the Lord. Our allegiance to His instructions shows up in the way we treat our neighbor, our family, and our church. God has good designs for us.

Notes

6
WHAT IF THE TRUTH HURTS?

"Speaking the truth in love, we are to grow up in every way into Him who is the head, into Christ."
— Ephesians 4:15

In things political, some stalwarts say they are emboldened to "speak truth to power." They will "tell it like it is" and "call a spade a spade." They will stand up and speak out. You see them on TV. They give speeches or lead protests or debate their foes. They aim to speak the truth, even if it hurts. Sometimes we admire that, as it shows real courage. Sometimes we cringe a bit, if they rather enjoy the hurt they're putting on people or if we disagree with the "truth" they're speaking/shouting.

Most of us know the challenge of challenging conversations. Most of us aren't good at it. It's hard to speak a correction or a *disagreement*. Be it in a congregation or in politics or in the family circle, it is not easy. We often just keep quiet rather that risk a spat, which may not turn out to be productive.

In many places, the Bible instructs us to get a voice and tell the truth. The prophet Ezekiel is plainly told that if he does not speak to warn the people of their evil ways, he will be held responsible (Ezekiel 3:17-19). We must not sit back and be silent in the face of wickedness. In Ephesians 4:15, St. Paul counsels us to "*speak the truth in love.*" There's the double mandate. The words we speak must be truthful plus loving. What an art that is. Some folks will speak the raw truth without love, and others will be nice but cowardly. What divine guidance we need to walk that balance beam. As a good parent tenderly corrects a child, or as a good child gently corrects an elderly parent, so in that spirit of love we are to proceed when the situation calls. Paul goes on to write that then "*we will grow up to become the mature body of Him who is the head, that is, Christ.*" It takes godly maturity. Many of us don't flow right into that. It's hard. Being mature is often a difficult path. The Lord will help us with this. We can grow into it. God bless you in that.

Notes

7
WHEN SHOULD WE BE NOT SO NICE?

"When I say to the wicked, 'O wicked man, you will surely die,' and you do not speak out to dissuade him from his ways, that wicked man will die for his sin, and I will hold you accountable for his blood."
— Ezekiel 33:8

Some of you around the country may not be familiar with the phrase "Minnesota Nice." It is used sometimes as a compliment, and sometimes as a pejorative. We all like folks to be polite — usually. In Minnesota and in the modern western world, high value is placed on MYOB ("Mind Your Own Business"). Ever since the 60s, it's "different strokes for different folks" and "whatever" — and for those who desire biblical backing: "don't judge." Most Americans love that Bible verse. You're supposed to be "nice", meaning easy-going and tolerant. That "niceness'" does not include offering corrections to others and voicing your <u>disagreements</u>. This is all good and normal, yes? Well, read on.

At a lunch gathering one day, a newcomer to Minnesota surprised the group by expressing dislike for our state. He rued the passivity and weakness of "Minnesota Nice." He thinks we need to stand up and speak out, not just go along with wrong. He coulda claimed Ezekiel 33:7-11 as his theme text. Ezekiel is told by the Lord, in no uncertain terms, that he must warn the wicked. He *must* do this. He must not remain silent. He must be a "*watchman*" on the tower who pays attention to evil and calls it out.

In the Old Testament, the prophets focused their calls for change on three main categories of evils:

1. Idolatry
2. Immorality
3. Injustice

These were the "Evil I's" that Ezekiel and others lambasted. These three have not gone extinct. You can check your news source daily and have plenty of case examples of those Evil I's.

So, unless you are that rare modern person who is too free with your warnings, the word to Ezekiel is also the word to us. We must hike up our courage and get our head out of the sand and lift our voice for what is right. Don't let evil waltz to victory. Edmund Burke said "All that is required for evil to triumph is for good men to do nothing." So, Christian: pray for the wisdom to know when to be "not nice."

Notes

8
WHAT IF I JUST CAN'T FORGIVE?

"As for you, you meant evil against me; but God meant it for good, to bring it about that many people should be kept alive, as they are today."
— Genesis 50:20

Most of you know the story of pretty-boy Joseph and his coat of many colors. It's a technicolor story: vivid and rich. Daddy's favorite son, and a man void of humility, Joseph is hated by his brothers. Getting a chance one day, they sell him as a slave to a passing caravan of merchants on camels. Joseph ends up down in Egypt. Years later, Joseph and his brothers meet again. He has risen to the role of governor in Egypt, and they are lowly foreigners seeking bread to survive from famine. Expecting Joseph's wrath for their dastardly deed years before, they instead receive *forgiveness*! Joseph is down-right Christ-like to his wicked brothers. Genesis 50:15-21 is exceptional: a model of grace.

How in the world could he forgive them? What made the reconciliation possible, when the natural human response would be vengeance? While his brothers clearly had it coming to them, somehow Joseph forgave. Clearly, there's a God-thing going on.

– 16 –

1. The brothers bring up God, and appeal to Joseph to see them as *"servants of the God of your father."* That may have helped.
2. Additionally, they bow and grovel. Remorse and repentance are an appropriate step.
3. Joseph is a gentle and kindly man, who *"wept when they spoke to him."* The Holy Spirit must have softened Joseph's heart.
4. Mainly though, I'd say that the Lord had given Joseph a divine double-vision. He was enabled to see that *"they meant it for evil, but God meant it for good."* In addition to seeing his life on the plain earthly level, Joseph was given the Godly bifocals to see that above the human story, the Lord also had a plan. More was going on than meets the eye.

Faith empowers us to see the hand of God at work in and with the human actions. Pray for heavenly help with how you see life. The wrongs done to you may be used by God to bring about a blessing later. Many a time, God's vision can free us up for forgiveness and reconciliation. Will you give those bifocals a try today?

Notes

9
DO YOU EVER JUST WANT TO DIE?

"For me to live is Christ, and to die is gain"
— Philippians 1:21

Alas, sometimes people find themselves in a situation where they are not sure whether it's better to live or to die. On most all of our pleasant and prosperous days in this very blessed nation, we just cruise on with life. Often with little depth of awareness, we go about our days with things to do and places to go and people to see. We're quite occupied with the doings of existence. That's the normal state of affairs. One could say that we are normally blissfully ignorant. But it's not always that way. On some occasions there will come an off-ramp from easy street and we will be face to face with our mortality. If the situation is grim enough, we may wonder if _death_ might be preferable. I have friends faced with whether to trudge on with painful cancer treatments long-term, or to "get their affairs in order." Perhaps you know folks in that situation as well.

The prospect of death is on the mind of St. Paul in Philippians 1:21-26. He sits in a prison cell — probably in martyr-producing Rome — with plenty of service scars accumulated, a legion of opponents out to get him, and a possible execution looming. Death may be near, and because of his assurance of the resurrection in Christ, Paul almost longs for it. His "*desire is to depart and be with Christ.*" He is "*hard-pressed*" on earth, so the heavenly banquet is quite inviting. Paul knows that death is not the end for the Christian, it's a promotion!

Yet while we "*remain in the flesh*" there is valuable work to be done. You can sense Paul's tilt toward staying on earth for now, 'cuz he's got good to do. There is "*fruitful labor*" for him, that is "*necessary on your account.*" For Paul and for us — as long as God gives us breath, in ways large or small — we are in the employ of the King of Love. As Paul puts it in Romans 14:8, "*Whether we live or whether we die, we are the Lord's.*" We know not what the future holds, but we know who holds the future. In good times or in bad, one day at a time, we live for Christ. In this life and the next — in today and in tomorrow — we glory in Jesus.

Notes

10
WHAT ARE YOU TRYING TO ACHIEVE?

"I press on toward the goal for the prize of the upward call of God in Christ Jesus."
— Philippians 3:14

What is it, do you figure, that most Americans are trying to achieve? All of the effort and activity of our years is toward what end? If we're straining toward a "touchdown," what is it? Many folks might think they've "made it" based on income level and possession acquisitions or number of years lived and key family markers achieved. That's the goal line for boatloads of people. It's not quite as crass as "he who dies with the most toys wins," but almost. Their goal line isn't too different than a squirrel's: a good chase around the tree, a few nuts to eat, and a comfy nest to rest in. With that some are satisfied. They have their *goals* in life, and they're earthy.

Such rank materialism was not Paul's idolatry. For years, his pursuit was personal righteousness. As Saul of Tarsus prior to his conversion, his life aim was building up his holiness rating. He was an exceptionally religious man, and had earned all the meritorious medals to win high honors among the upstanding citizens. He was no slacker; his life was exemplary. He was hall of fame caliber in his piety.

Despite that, Paul came to see those things as "*rubbish,*" as he terms it in Philippians 3:8. Not only would he consider material possessions junk, he considered character merit badges junk, too. He would do no touchdown dance for fleeting earthly accomplishments. His life pursuit was not prestige, not possessions, not popularity. An eternal relationship with His Savior is the only goal line that Paul will "*press on*" toward and "*strain ahead*" for. It is his sole "*prize to win.*"

Like Paul, we would be wise to pursue the goal line that is not futile. Both the material goods of life and the praise of our fellows just does not last. You will be carried out in a box, and you will not be long remembered. That's the honest truth regarding your physical existence. Rather, seek Christ. Choose the goal line that is eternal. As someone said: "That man is no fool who gives what he cannot keep to gain what he cannot lose." Living for our own glory does not get you to the victory party.

Notes

11
Do We Humans Run The World?

> *"I am the Lord, and there is no other, besides me there is no God; I gird you, though you do not know me."*
>
> — Isaiah 45:5

Sometimes we think we're in charge; or at least have things figured out. We humans are smart; and we love to make sense of the world and have some control of how things will turn out. However, it becomes clear now and again that we're not that smart, nor are we in charge. We are flawed and fleeting creatures. Only the Lord is sovereign. As someone put it: "There is only one God; and you're not it." We do well to acknowledge our place in the universe, and to have a grateful _humility_ about life. Indeed, it may take a load off you to realize that you are not responsible for running the world! God is still God.

What a lesson on this Isaiah lays out in chapter 45! As the beaten and besieged people of Israel fret about their future, and try to figure out what political alliances will benefit them, the prophet Isaiah announces that there will indeed be a brighter day ahead. Isaiah expresses hope about the nation's future. He is not a gloom and doom guy. But the stunner is: the positive change will come via the brute tyrant of Persia: Cyrus! "What's that you say?! Israel's oppressor will be the one to bring about something good?! A foreign king, nasty Cyrus, will be an instrument in God's hand?!" Isaiah shocks the people with this logic-defying news. He makes it clear that God is God; the Lord is sovereign, and it is His prerogative to do as He sees fit. Israel would never choose to have their rescue via the dreaded Persian, but it shall be so, says the Lord.

What does this mean for us today? Don't try to box God in! Don't try to limit His hand. Despite our many advancements, and our progress in technology and government and knowledge, yet the Almighty says "*I am the Lord and there is no other.*" Though He surprise us, or even confound us, He is in charge. He may pull an upset and disturb our expectations. We remain mere mortals. Would you say that's good for us?

Notes

12
DO YOU WANT JUSTICE?

"For we hold that a man is justified by faith apart from works of law."
— Romans 3:28

When Luther posted his 95 theses in 1517, the core issue was justification. The Church split and history was forever changed because of *"justification by faith."* People were very concerned about how to get right with God. Now, 500 years later, no one is riled up about justification, but instead about <u>justice</u>. Papers are written and speeches are given and protests are held focused on the matter of justice. Justice, not justification, is the desire. Folks want things "put right"; they want what's coming to them. They think.

A humble soul, aware of his/her own culpability in our human mess, might quake at the thought of true and divine justice. That could turn out badly for a good many of us. Indeed, St. Paul says in Romans 3:23 that *"all have sinned and fallen short of the glory of God."* That being the case, you better hope that the Almighty has a kinder offer than giving you what you deserve! If you hunger for justice, but in fact are part of the injustice of earthly life, how will that go down?

Have you heard these little definitions?

- Justice is getting what you deserve;
- Mercy is not getting what you deserve; and
- Grace is getting better than you deserve!"

Rings true, does it not? At least for us sinners. Only the blind and arrogant person would want the Almighty to "give 'em what is coming to them." With no hope of justifying ourselves in the eyes of a righteous God, Luther and all Christians are beyond elated that the Lord is gracious. "Saved by grace!".... not "demanding our due" is the Christian cry. We are eternally grateful that Christ brings mercy to idiots and sinners like us.

Now, of course there is great need for justice in the courts and on the human level, and we are wise to strive for it. Humanity is much handicapped when the scales of justice are rigged. Both justice and justification are keys to human flourishing.

Notes

13
ARE MY DAYS NUMBERED?

"So teach us to number our days that we may get a heart of wisdom."
— Psalm 90:12

In recent years there have been ads for a special bed, where consumers can dial in their own preferred "sleep number." Apparently each person has a number; with this bed you can pick that number and get a great night's sleep. Allow your mind to jump now to a weightier "sleep number." Fact is, you and every person shall "fall asleep" (as we euphemize death). You shall take a dirt-nap. You will lay down and not awake in this life. We don't know when that day will be. It could be today. It could be years and years from now. But there is a "sleep number"; a number of days you will live, and a day on which you will die. I suppose you could say that the date on your tombstone (e.g. 2018) is your "sleep number." No one gets out alive, and on some calendar day you shall "fall asleep."

Christians are honest about this death business. We don't live in denial, pretending that we'll never "fall asleep." We are honest about death, but not morbid. We are aware of our _mortality_. We do not "*grieve as those who have no hope*" as St. Paul put it. Rather, we trust in — yes, even eagerly anticipate — our promotion to life eternal by the victory of Jesus. All who fall asleep in Jesus shall awaken to life eternal! Just as you are not afraid to shut your eyes and go to sleep at night, the Christian is not afraid of the final sleep. It's like, "See ya in the morning." Not afraid to die, we now can really live. We take no days for granted. We are fully aware that our days are numbered, and thus precious and passing. We are prepping for paradise; we are practicing for the party without end.

Psalm 90 tells us to "*number our days, that we may gain a heart of wisdom.*" Use each day as the unique occasion that it is, a chance to thank and praise, serve and obey your good Lord. The animals take no thought about tomorrow; are unaware of any "sleep number." We humans are different, intended for far more than mere physical existence. Use this day well, knowing that Jesus has a place reserved for you.

Notes

14
WILL WE HUMANS EVER WISE UP?

"The fear of the Lord is the beginning of wisdom; a good understanding have all those who practice it. His praise endures forever!"
— Psalm 111:10

"What in the world is wrong with people?!" Can't you just hear that? Or maybe you'd utter it yourself. The human story seems like a long blooper reel some days. Good golly, miss Molly, it's an awful mess. We mangle our priorities. We mistreat each other. We mar God's masterpiece creation. We spew lies and we besmirch our neighbors. We neglect the elderly. We continue our racism. Well…. one could go on, but you get it. You know it. We humanoids are repeatedly fools and sinners.

Christians know that the shed blood of Jesus and the eternal grace of God is our only hope for all this brokenness. We just plain are not smart enough nor good enough to rescue ourselves.

Thus, it's only a secondary blessing when God's Word lauds *wisdom*. The truth and benevolence of the Lord's teachings to us do not save, but they do bless. Our heavenly Father has heavenly counsel throughout the Scripture that is given in love. Be it called wisdom or precepts or ordinances or laws or parables or commandments, the Lord has a lot to teach us. (For a whole huge exaltation of God's written Word, see magnificent Psalm 119.) A small tribute to it is in Psalm 111: "*The fear of the Lord is the beginning of wisdom; a good understanding have all those who practice it.*"

Let's peek into that briefly. First, there's the "*fear of the Lord is the beginning of wisdom*" phrase. We must begin with the humility to know that we are not God. We bow before Him in full awareness of our errors and in grateful realization of His majesty. We silence ourselves in awe of the Almighty. To do otherwise is to be air-headedly arrogant. The first step in learning is to be willing to be taught, to know that you are under the tutelage of one who is greater. Without that "*fear*" / respect, we are refusing to learn. So instead, "down with foolishness." Let's wise up and listen.

Are we willing to trust God; that "*all who follow his precepts have good understanding*"? It is such a modern Western mantra that we are to "do our own thing" and "be your own person" and "follow your dreams" and etc. We are in love with self-invention and individuality. We often accept no authority. With that as our thick cultural milieu, will we actually subject our wills to another — even if that other is God Himself? Maybe. To think that we know best — that our little slice of history as white, well-off, Westerners is the benchmark for truth — is plain elitism. It's blind folly. Down with foolishness, and up with the truth that stands the test of time. So let's test His truth and practice His wisdom, that holds in every time and place. If we do, we will join the Psalmist in exclaiming: "*To Him belongs eternal praise.*"

Notes

15
WHAT DO YOU THINK OF PARENTAL AUTHORITY?

"Master, we toiled all night and took nothing. But at your word I will let down the nets."
— Luke 5:5)

When should a person obey someone else? Is there a place for "just because"? Is it not out-moded and debunked here in the 21st century to have a hierarchical relationship where one person is subject to the authority of another? Modern Western humans are big into independence and self-determination, so to propose a place for authority and <u>obedience</u> is to mess with a sacred cow of our culture. Let's think about this, by way of an event from the life of Jesus long ago and far away.

In Luke 5, a phenom named Jesus had just finished teaching a crowd by a lake, having borrowed a fishing boat. When He was finished, He asked the fisherman, Peter, to toss out the nets for a catch. Peter and company were done for the day and were bushed and frustrated, having been skunked after long hours of fishing. The response of Peter to Jesus is striking: *"Master, we toiled all night and took nothing! But at your word I will let down the nets."* So,

Peter does as Jesus asked, "because you say so." Peter submitted his will to Jesus' will. It didn't make full sense to Peter, nor did he feel like it, but he did it.

Is there an appropriate parallel here regarding parenting? Jesus was indeed the Master, but we humans are not Jesus, eh? We may agree that obedience to our Lord Jesus is good, but parents are human and they're not Jesus. Parents are not God and not infallible, so they would be wise to recognize that they are *not* the highest authority. Yet I suggest that these two authority and obedience experiences do have a similarity.

A child has a built-in authority called "mom" and/or "dad." A child is young and inexperienced, but is provided with the protection and wisdom of his/her parent. God blesses children by giving them parents, whose job it is to care for them physically, developmentally, emotionally and spiritually. A wise and loving parent does what is best for the child, and does not wait for the child's approval. As the relationship of trust and love grows over the years, the child learns that mom and/or dad are trustworthy, so that authority is granted and need not be forced. This healthy dynamic will produce some situations where the child obeys not just if it makes immediate sense to him/her — and not just if he/she feels like obeying — but "because you say so." Similar to our faith response to Jesus, the response is "I know that you love me and that you act for my benefit, so I will do as you want because you say so."

Children who learn to trust their parents are learning to trust God. Children who learn to obey their parents are learning to obey God. Parents should use this authority carefully and prayerfully, realizing the full weight of this responsibility.

Notes

16
ARE WE MORE THAN PHYSICAL?

"We look not to the things that are seen but to the things that are unseen; for the things that are seen are transient, but the things that are unseen are eternal."
— 2 Corinthians 4:18

Some things are indeed obvious: the nose on your face, the cause of drunkenness, the need for rain. Physical and measurable realities are seen, obviously. Unless one is a total materialist, we humans are also aware of unseen things. We have gotten schooled on the reality and power of many invisible things: gravity, electricity, wind, radio waves, etc. The natural world has come to terms with these. Can we also be enlightened on unseen / non-obvious *spiritual* things? You cannot measure a pound of love or take a picture of justice, yet most folks are convinced that they are real and are vital. Although humans are animals in some senses, most of us realize that there are spiritual dimensions of our nature that mere physicality and instinct do not capture.

It is of this unseen, spiritual realm that St. Paul writes in 2 Corinthians 4: *"We look not to things that are seen but to things that are unseen."* Christ-followers pin our hearts and build our lives on a reality outside mere physical existence. Though spiritual realities are not obvious to all, Christians are empowered by God's truth: that kindness pays, that love wins, that Jesus rose, that we are not accidents, that prayers are heard, that life is a gift, that heaven is real. These things cannot be proven. They are not obvious to all. They are "*unseen*" with the naked eye. Only when the Lord grants to us the eyes of faith do we live our lives devoted to those unseen things.

Paul wisely tells us that "*the things that are seen are transient*" (v. 19). That includes us and our bodies. It may sound insulting to say that you are a transient — as in "homeless person" — but that's the cold hard truth physically. We come, and we go, unless there is a God who beat death on our behalf. In Jesus "*the things that are unseen are eternal.*" We aim high, and stake our lives on noble realities that cannot be proven. Though it be not obvious, it is life-giving.

Notes

17
IS IT OK TO RELAX?

"Jesus said 'The kingdom of God is as if a man should scatter seed upon the ground, and should sleep and rise night and day, and the seed should sprout and grow, he knows not how.'"
— Mark 4:26-27

My sweet bride loves romantic comedies. In one of those, entitled "While you were Sleeping", a plot that is both crazy and lovely unfolds for an unwitting Sandra Bullock. While one guy is in a coma, a whole life-changing series of events takes place. He doesn't know a thing about it, and she didn't mastermind it. Somehow it all comes round right. Hollywood doesn't deal in Divine <u>Providence</u>, so they'd explain it as dumb luck. (People like me, who married way up, and have had so many life pieces "fall in place," are ever-grateful for the Lord's invisible work.)

We who trust in the Lord do believe in and give honor to Divine Providence. "*The Lord shall provide*" has been among our tenets since Abraham on Mt. Moriah. We have faith, that even if unbeknownst to us, our good God is at work to bring about blessings and rescues. Our confidence is not in ourselves, in our merit, performance or pure intentions. Nope. Our trust is in the Lord alone.

I hope you find this truth truly freeing. What wonderful relief it is to know that how things will turn out isn't all on you! God wants to use us, true. God calls us to join Him as instigators and distributors of blessing, true. We have our part to play (so don't be a slacker). But to say that it's all up to us is untrue. God is God: He is at work to bestow life, health and salvation, even when we are asleep. So sleep tight; don't carry the weight of the world on your puny shoulders. That's the Lord's job.

In Jesus' parable in Mark 4 He tells us that the kingdom of God is underway and will grow *"while you are sleeping,"* night and day, though we know not how. I love that. I don't have to lay awake and worry, don't need to fret about outcomes, don't have to live my days sweating. It's like the farmer: he does his part, then admires what God has built into seeds and soil and seasons. He need not yell at the plants to get with it. He need not pull on their heads to make them produce. God's got a plan; God's got the power. Isn't He just marvelous? (And it's not "lucky us," it's "blessed us!")

Notes

18

HOW MANY LOAVES DO YOU HAVE?

"Jesus said to them 'how many loaves do you have? Go and see.' And when they had found out, they said 'Five, and two fish.'"
— Mark 6:38

There are many ways to mine the riches of Scripture and to come up with beneficial results. A seeking soul can find salutary nourishment. One method for Bible study is just to hone in on the questions that are printed. For example: *"Who do you say that I am?"* (Mark 16:15) or *"Am I my brother's keeper?"* (Genesis 4:9). Good questions instigate valuable answers. A well-placed question is powerful.

In Mark 6, in the feeding of the 5,000, a person could have several key takeaways. Such as:

- Jesus is compassionate for the masses;
- Jesus feeds bodies and souls; and
- Jesus has divine power.

All these are true; and we can draw inspiration and strength from them. Note now also the key question Jesus asks His disciples: *"How many loaves do you have?"* He wants them thinking about what they can do in the midst

— 36 —

of a large need. He doesn't want them grounded with the common poverty-mentality that thinks, "We got nothing," "We aren't up to this," or "Tsk tsk, it sure is too bad." He wants them to do possibility-thinking — to brainstorm, to dream big. Jesus has told them that "*with God all things are possible*," and now they get a chance to step up and do something big. Their only food resource that day was five loaves and two fish. It wasn't much, but it was presented to the Lord. Lo and behold, Jesus could do great things with their meager fare! They needed to have a willing *faith*. If they brought what they had to Jesus, He could do mighty things with it.

Some theologians warn of "realized eschatology" pipe dreams, that some Christians are naively Utopian. They say we shouldn't fall into "the power of positive thinking" and assume that we can bring in the Kingdom of God. OK — we are not the Messiah, that's for sure. Yet, I'd say that most Christians aim too low. We can use what we have to let Jesus accomplish godly signs and wonders. Whether the issue in front of us is hunger, like that day, or abuse or loneliness or crime, we can think of some contribution we can bring. (What's in your wallet?)

Notes

19
IS PROSPERITY A TEST?

"Then the Lord said to Moses, 'behold, I will rain bread from heaven for you; and the people shall go out and gather a day's portion every day, that I may prove them, whether they will walk in my law or not.'"
— Exodus 16:4

Heavens to Betsy, do we have it good. For most all of us Betsys and Bobbys, here in the 21st century West, we live like queens and kings. We have vastly more technology and prosperity than royalty through the ages. Even their large castles would need major upgrades to be acceptable to us. Right? They didn't have running water nor HVAC nor electricity, much less our beloved internet. So, this is all to say that we are prosperous. We live plush. I'm not knocking that. I'm as addicted to my modern conveniences and comfortable life as the next guy. (Though it's true that I still use a flip-phone.)

Occasionally, I do step back and wonder: is our well-off status a blessing or a curse? Is it possible that God is too good to us? Could our _prosperity_ be a test? That's how it is presented to Moses and the Israelites in Exodus 16. Having heard the complaints of the people regarding how tough they had it post-Egypt, the LORD decides to shower them

– 38 –

daily with food. He will rain down bread from heaven (i.e. manna). "*In this way I will test them and see whether they will follow my instructions.*" God's largess was a test. They hadn't obeyed Him in lean times, so now maybe they'd do better via easier times. (Spoiler alert: it didn't work.)

I suppose it's true that whether we are scuffling along or are living the high-life, it's a test. Our days and years are an ongoing opportunity to see how we handle it. I think that either grave poverty or excess riches would be a trying spiritual challenge. And I'd guess we'd all prefer the upper-class test (even though Christianity does better in poorer countries than in wealthy). Whatever your lot in life, pray and plan to be a faithful steward who follows God's instructions. When you have the prosperity test, the correct answer is: generosity.

Notes

20

Isn't The World Dreadful?

"There they are, overwhelmed with dread; for God is present in the company of the righteous."
— Psalm 14:5

I sometimes tell my wife that the news hour is the "anxiety hour." Day after day the reporters sock it to us on how dreadful the world is. You've gotta either have thick skin or a strong heart to pay attention to the world's news. What's leading the news today as you read this? Let me guess: violence, disaster and corruption. The news slams you around for 29 minutes, filled with gloom and doom and things to worry about — and then they try to soften the blow in the last minute with a cute story about a dog. They may not be all the way to "the sky is falling," but they push you that direction.

No wonder the nation is anxious. No wonder there is more insecurity than ever. To quote the Psalmist: "*There they are, overwhelmed with dread.*" Many in our dear nation feel <u>*discouraged*</u>, and they dread the future. They think it's all heading south. Now, our era is no more dreadful than when the Psalms were written — just think of those wars

– 40 –

and famines and plagues — but an honest person would admit, "Yup, there's a lot of lousy all the way around." When Psalm 14 uses words like "*corrupt,*" "*vile,*" or "*evildoers,*" we get it. Life on earth is majorly messy.

    I will not now tell you, "Aw, it's not so bad really." I won't be Pollyanna and tell you to smile and think positive and count your blessings. Sometimes that can help, but we need more. And thank the Lord, we have more. We have a rock and a refuge, One who rescues and restores. We will not fear — at least not to the worldly point of anxiety and hysteria. We may be short-term pessimists — as there is plenty of dreadful dissolution — but we are long-term optimists. Christ the King shall reign forever in love. Though the days be very stormy, we know that there is a beautiful port ahead. Therefore, as the Psalm continues: "*...let Jacob rejoice and Israel be glad.*" Though troubles be great, God is greater!

Notes

21
DOES GOOD BEHAVIOR PAY?

"Now, Israel, hear the decrees and laws I am about to teach you. Follow them so that you may live and may go in and take possession of the land the Lord is giving you."
— Deuteronomy 4:1

Not to be too crass here, but does *morality* pay? If we live clean, is there a reward? (And I don't mean pie in the sky.) Likewise, if we disobey, is there corresponding punishment? Well, let me try two disclaimers.

1. Such a methodology to obedience is contrary to what the Lord wants. We are not to do what God commands in order to thereby earn goodies from God. That'd be low — like giving your girlfriend chocolates in order to get kisses. Such ignoble cause and effect is not commendable. The Almighty is not bought off with bribery.
2. A gracious heavenly Father is generous to all, not just to the obedient. Jesus told us that God *"sends rain on the righteous and on the unrighteous"* (Matthew 5:5). The Lord grants food even to the rat-finks.

So now, having named two factors that might weigh into the "no" column, I'll risk being unorthodox by saying "yes, sorta." Good behavior pays. It doesn't always pay neatly with a ratio of 1:1, but it makes life go better. We could go so far as say: "Obey God, or else." We wouldn't pitch it that way, but it has some truth.

    Throughout the Old Testament, like in Deuteronomy, there are causal consequences to obedience or lack thereof. A very basic and oft-repeated biblical theology is the "if / then" dynamic. "If" Israel obeys, "then" God will be pleased. "If" the Lord's laws are followed, "then" life will be well. "If" the people rebel, "then" disasters will come. Cause and effect is clearly the m.o. Now, we shouldn't get simplistic with this, and assume there's a divine "tit for tat." (The sufferings of righteous Job, and the crucifixion of sinless Christ cut that cord!) We must not go to "you are hurting so you musta done bad." Nonetheless, in general, as a rule, as a group, we do "*reap what we sow*" as St. Paul puts it. If you want a better world, be a better person. If you want less pain and heartache, live life God's way. He gives us His law in love, as a gift. You are free to disobey it, but not free of the repercussions. Go a little easier on yourself and your neighbors, and do life God's way.

Notes

22
WHAT ARE YOU AFRAID OF?

"Let not your hearts be troubled; neither let them be afraid."
— John 14:27

Humans have fears. Life has things to be afraid of. Many people have standard fears: heights, dark alleys, infirmity, poverty. Kids often fear strangers, loud noises, monsters. Tough-guy Indiana Jones was afraid of snakes. Current national fears might include terrorism, economic collapse and political opponents. (I get letters from both political parties, and they both appeal to fear of the other. They know they can motivate you by fear, of those "extremists.") How about you? Do you know your *fears*? Fear can be very powerful — a driving force in how we live our lives. For some, a life motivation is fear of failure, and for others it's the opposite: fear of success. There are plenty of fears that propel Americans into certain lifestyles. Think now a bit about these two: FOMO and FOBI.

"FOMO" is Fear Of Missing Out. This is fear that we'll be out of it, out of the loop, not included. This fear keeps some people glued to their social media or the news or their in-group. It drives overextended lives and lack of sleep and insecurity. Those with FOMO may chase experiences or information or money or bucket lists, driven to not miss out.

"FOBI" is Fear Of Blending In. Our culture loves the new, the unique, the special. Since the 50s we have adored the rebel and opposed conformity. Many want to "do it my way" and stand out from the crowd. Not blending in gets you fame, or on the news, or at least a mention by some. FOBI seems to be especially American. Many of our young people know that they are special, but are dismayed that they haven't been discovered yet. They sure don't want to just blend in with everybody else..

One of the most repeated teachings in the Good Book is "*Do Not be Afraid.*" The Lord is anti-fear. Fear is a negative emotion; but Jesus tells us to "*fear not.*" He wants us to find our deep and eternal security where it can only be found: in His love. To be in relationship with Jesus, the Lord of love and Victor over death, is to have the blessed assurance that:

> *...neither death nor life, nor angels nor principalities, nor things present nor things to come, nor powers, nor height nor depth, nor anything in all creation will be able to separate us from the love of God in Christ Jesus.*
> — Romans 8:38

He's got you. He grants the Christian the peace of God that earth cannot destroy. If not even death can beat the Lord... fear not.

Notes

23
IS THE FLAT-EARTH-SOCIETY GROWING?

"After this I looked, and lo, in heaven an open door!"
— Revelation 4:1

Centuries ago, it was common knowledge that the earth was flat. Everybody thought that. Then they didn't. What was previously accepted was short-sighted and wrong. It turned out that ships would not sail off the edge and plunge into oblivion. Humans found out that the earth was round, not flat. Thanks, Aristotle! In our century it seems that there's a neo-Flat Earth Society. More people have gotten to thinking that this earth is it; that all that exists is what meets the naked eye. (OK, they would add what the telescope and microscope can see, too.) They see no spiritual nor eternal realities, no God. Not to blame John Lennon and his song *Imagine*, but perhaps you know the lyrics: "Imagine there's no heaven, it's easy if you try; No hell below us; above us only sky." It's kind of the atheists' theme song. If more and more folks are secular materialists, they are today's flat-earthers.

Allow me to spar with them and advocate for a "3-D" approach to our days instead. Rather than the flat and limited view of life, Christ-followers have a deeper and broader and higher vision. We have _faith_.

1. We have deep roots / a firm foundation / a spiritual grounding for our years. We know that we didn't create ourselves nor gift ourselves. We are intentionally created, our feet are on solid ground and under us are the everlasting arms. There is a God who is supreme, and we are esteemed by Him, not vainly self-esteemed

2. We are legion / surrounded by God's people / included in a historic community. We are not alone vs. the world or orphaned in the universe. We have brothers and sisters in the love of Christ all around the globe. We don't have to go at life alone. We have allies in more than the cause d'jour. We are tied to something much bigger than the supreme "me."

3. We have an eternal horizon. It's no dead-end ahead for us. Death is but a comma, not a period. We have an inextinguishable joy, not dependent on the vagaries of earth. Our reservations are in at the heavenly banquet.

Our dancing shoes are gonna smile and fly — not 'cuz we dream it so, but because Jesus wins it so. Our existence is deeper, broader and higher.

Go 3-D! Don't settle for the grim grayness of those no-hope flat-earthers. As Revelation 4:1 puts it, take a look and see: heaven is open! Thanks, Jesus!

Notes

24

ARE PEOPLE STUPID?

"Like a dog that returns to his vomit is a fool that repeats his folly"
— Proverbs 26:11

Criminy, Chris, this is not a nice question. (The verse in Proverbs 26:11 isn't a nice one, either. It did grab your attention and made you go "yuck", though.) The question here sounds sour and dour, or even downright mean-spirited. Depending on the mood you're in today, maybe you'd say, "People are actually sweet and smart, and just make mistakes sometimes." You'd have a pretty rosy and gracious view of your fellow-humans. Or you might say, "You bet your sweet bippy those #!*^ humans do monstrous dumbassery." You might be rather miffed at those blasted humanoids. I think that a calm, settled mind would land in-between those, and own up to the reality that we humans can be brilliant and also can be idiots. There's a mountain of evidence for both. Neither would be a molehill.

If you'd like to de-stupidize yourself, and help others with their smarts too, the good Lord has help available on that. He wants to assist us with *How to Think*. That's the title of a big-selling book by Dr. Alan Jacobs. Jacobs, painfully aware of our world-at-odds, offers reasonable and academic advice on better thinking. He wants us to refrain from thinking errors such as:

- "Group-think" / "echo chamber" of listening only to like-minded voices;
- Knee-jerk "refute mode," when you plan your response rather than listen to an opposing point of view;
- Use of pejoratives and dichotomies, which we may think are rather smart, but are not wise thinking; and
- "Confirmation bias," which filters our thinking so that we only listen to what already fits our worldview; etc.

Jacobs and his book have some good tips for lessening our stupidity and increasing our peace-ability. His new book has benefit, but our old Book — available in every language and on every continent — is the mother lode for us. Be it the book of *wisdom* (Proverbs) or the timeless teachings throughout the Book, the Bible can implant some artificial intelligence that works against our natural stupidity. Not to say we are dog-like, but we do return to gross errors time and again. We could just suffer through those mistakes as in the "school of hard knocks," but why not instead focus on God's Word, the "school of soft knocks"? Both Christians and secularists would agree: we could use help with learning smarter ways. Up with wisdom!

Notes

25

Do You Have Enemies?

"Lead me, O Lord, in thy righteousness because of my enemies; make thy way straight before me."
— Psalm 5:8

You are probably not paranoid. Your daily life flows along pretty peacefully, eh? No one is out to get you. At least, I sure hope not. For those who aren't living in a war zone, a crime-infested neighborhood or are being bullied at school or work, you maybe could not make a list of your <u>enemies</u>. Good. You live in peace and safety most all of the time.

That's not how it was for David. Both prior to and during his kingship in Israel, David had many foes. Read the Psalms and you are struck by how many of them are pleas to God to rescue him from his enemies. It's not a couple here and there. "*Save and deliver me from those who are out to destroy my life*" or something of that gist is repeatedly uttered. Stress and strife are his regular and unwanted companions.

So, what does that have to do with us? If you can't name any enemies, are all those Psalm prayers irrelevant to you? I say they're not. I say that you do in fact have enemies. (Am I paranoid?) I could say this just spiritually, and that's often how I appropriate those Psalms. The non-physical enemies — greed, malice, jealousy, despair, complacency and such — are regularly out to get us. They want to undo us, to get under our skin, to darken our days, to separate us from our Father. I bet you experience that too. So OK, that's bearable, and hopefully beneficial to know. Our inner state faces opposition most every day. We live in spiritual warfare.

Let me go on to say that we have actual flesh and blood enemies too. There are plenty of people who oppose Christians, plus some people who will treat you badly, on purpose. That's part of the earthly experience. It may not be as outfront as the hateful neighbor or the political adversaries in the R vs. D scrum, but enemies do exist. This could be at work, or in the extended family, or out there on the streets. Don't expect everyone to be lovey-dovey. Even if your personal world is at peace, do remember those who are in battle zones or persecution nations.

And do pray and practice that whole "*love your enemies*" strategy that Jesus teaches us. That takes a whole lot of work, but I'm just giving you a heads-up.

Notes

26
ARE YOUR CHILDREN YOURS?

"Behold, children are a heritage from the Lord."
— Psalm 127:3

Your perspective can make a huge difference. How you see a situation may determine your response. This old poem can help you with this concept:

Two men looked out from prison bars,
One saw mud, the other, stars.

Their outer realities were the same, but their inner realities — their perspectives — were in stark contrast. Similarly, one person may see an interruption in the day as a problem, and another person could see it as an opportunity. One person may see himself as the owner of his possessions, and another person could see himself as the steward of his possessions, with God as the real owner. That different perspective probably results in a different way of handling his stuff.

To apply this now to <u>*parenting*</u>... is your child yours? Is he or she your possession? Are you the owner of your child, or the trustee of God's child? A Christian tries to cultivate that latter perspective. If your child is God's child, entrusted to your care and keeping for awhile, what does that mean for you? First, you have then a holy responsibility, and are inspired to be heaven's emissary for your beloved boy or girl. Second, you are liberated from what could be a crushing weight of responsibility if you thought it was all on you, alone, to love and develop that young life. God is always beside you, supporting and guiding. Christians should try to parent as trustees. Parents: your child is a gift, from the Lord, placed into your hands.

One of the biblical accounts that pictures this for us is from 1 Samuel, chapter 1. Hannah and Elkanah, who have been childless for so many years, are finally granted a son, Samuel. Hannah knows that this boy is a gift, an answer to prayer, and so she dedicates Samuel to the Lord. Samuel will live as a servant of God, growing up to become the priest who anoints Israel's first king. From an early age, Samuel is given a divine purpose. He was not the possession of Hannah and Elkanah, for them to own and control. He was a heavenly gift.

How does this perspective on parenting shape us? What blessings can grow from this way of seeing our children? What responsibilities and assurances do we feel when we see our parenting jobs as that of trustee rather than owner?

Notes

27

CAN WE BE SPIRITUAL BUT NOT RELIGIOUS?

"Abide in me, and I in you. As the branch cannot bear fruit by itself, unless it abides in the vine, neither can you, unless you abide in me."
— John 15:4

An option that has really grown popular in our lifetime is for people to be "*spiritual* but not religious." That means they some want inner goodness and long-term meaning, without being tied to a religion. They don't want to be shallow materialists — as in just physical creatures — but they eschew the rituals and restrictions of religion. For those who know the warts and weaknesses of religion, we might sympathize with this desire. One would be free of set doctrines and commandments, plus free of human entanglements (i.e. "spiritual" is individual, while "religious" is communal). A spiritual man can just dump smelly Elroy Olson, while the religious man has to figure out how to get along with Elroy in the congregation. The individual freedom of "spiritual but not religious" is perfect for a supremely individualistic culture. You don't even have to get out of bed on Sunday mornings.

You're getting the sense that I'm not for this. It strikes me as selfish and short-sighted. Let me try to bend the question this way: "Can you have fruit without a tree?" Well.... I have apples but no apple tree. Someone else grows my apples; I just buy them. Can this work in the spiritual realm? Can someone else do the service and sacrifice, the fellowship and discipline, and I just get the goods? Well.... a productive tree produces enough for others, right? If the "*fruit of the Spirit is love, joy, peace, patience*" etc, then those good things benefit / are shared with lots of folks. God is good, and the fruit can be bountiful.

These days there are many secularists who like our Christian fruit. They share with us a high value on love, peace, mercy, compassion, etc. They give speeches and hold rallies for these values. You might say they love our fruit, but don't want our tree. They want Jesus' values, but not Jesus. They think these are human ideals that can be manufactured just fine by humans. Perhaps they believe that people have a higher consciousness within them, and that we can evolve into these values on our own. This is "post-Christian" spirituality. I fear that it will be like cut flowers: beautiful, but they won't last. Christians know that we are actually a mess inside, bent in our ourselves, and need divine help. Christ-followers admit that we need to "*abide in the vine to bear much fruit.*" We are committed to "spiritual and religious." So, believer, hang in there.

Notes

28
What's Your Dream?

> "But now the Lord my God has given me rest on every side; there is neither adversity nor misfortune. And so I purpose to build a house for the Name of the Lord my God."
> — 1 Kings 5:4-5

A lot of life is just necessity. You plug away and hoe your row because you have to. There are tasks that have to be done and there are deadlines that have to be met and there are bills that have to be paid. A bumper-sticker expressed it this way: "I owe, I owe, it's off to work I go." There's often a tyranny of necessity to daily life. Day by day we just do what needs to be done. (And this is often good, I dare say. A life of leisure and the pursuit of our dreams would not always turn out for good. The 21st century has massive discretionary time for a great many people; and many use it ignobly. Someone once said "idleness is the devil's workshop," eh.)

It doesn't have to be that way. Consider this: if you had ample time and money, what would you do with it? If the day comes and you retire — so you're not having to work for a living — what do you do then? Think about that. What's your dream? What do you do when you don't have to do anything?

The time came for King Solomon. As he said: "The Lord God has given me rest on every side, and there is no adversary nor disaster." He had made it. In your little kingdom, when there is rest, without adversary or disaster or necessity to constrain you.... Then what? Such freedom and opportunity that would be! The questions might be: What sort of legacy do you want to leave? How do you want to steward your days? What's your *purpose*? Solomon chose to build a temple for the Name of the Lord. It was a massive work of art; one of the Wonders of the ancient world. (Read all about it in 1 Kings 6, 7 & 8.) He really dreamed big.

Many people today with time and money build themselves a dream home or buy a yacht or travel the world. How 'bout you? The Christ-follower might dream differently. Could you volunteer your talents? Or send kids to camp? Or fund a missionary? Or write a book? Or invent a product? Or run for office? Or....... ? Dream on. Then make a plan with some action steps and some allies, and let 'er rip. The clock is ticking.

Notes

GOD QUESTIONS

Who is God & what is He up to?

Theology

29

WHAT SORT OF GOD DO WE HAVE?

"When the Spirit of truth comes, he will guide you into all the truth; for he will not speak on his own authority, but whatever he hears he will speak, and will declare to you the things that are to come."
— John 16:13

You know about Christmas: God took on flesh in Jesus. You know about Easter: God defeated death in Jesus. Our third major holy day as Christians is Pentecost. Many people don't know what it is about, although it is the indispensable part 3 in the drama of our salvation. The birth, life, death, and resurrection of Jesus would be just historical without Pentecost. They would be dates on the dusty calendar of human history, consigned to the good old days, unless the Lord should continue His work in our lives and hearts today. It is the Holy Spirit on the move — the life and power of Jesus ongoing — that enlightens and enlivens minds and hearts from age to age.

This confounds some. This truth of "*Trinity*" — that God's work is as Father, Son, and Holy Spirit — is beyond our cranial capacity to explain, but is the essential saving glory of the Lord. Today again we can marvel and rejoice in the fullness of what God has done for us. To omit any of the three-in-one would result in incompletion. Exult today in who God is.

Ponder again the fullness of God. He is your Father. He has created you and blessed you from the beginning. He showers gifts upon you out of His divine goodness. He provides for you and protects you and promises you His eternal love. What a God! Merciful and mighty is He!

He is also your Savior. He has left His throne on high to stoop low to rescue you. He would stop at nothing to win you. He would suffer the loss of His life to redeem yours. He would blow open the door of death for you. What a God! Merciful and mighty is He!

He is also your Counselor, ever-present instigator of faith and love. He stirs and prods, comforts and guides. He delivers to you daily the inner gifts of salvation: peace of mind, purpose of days, joy of life, wellspring of love, intimacy with God, assurance of heaven. "*God's love has been poured into our hearts by the Holy Spirit.*" What a God! Merciful and mighty is He!

Notes

30
Isn't God A Loser At Love?

> "*I spread out my hands all the day to a rebellious people, who walk in a way that is not good, following their own devices.*"
> — Isaiah 65:2

Some relationships are very one-sided. When one person is "all-in" — fully on board with love and devotion — and the other person is not, then that is a recipe for heartache. Think of the young man who wants to marry his gal, but she prefers to keep her options open. Think of the mother who steadfastly gives and gives for the good of her son, but he just does not reciprocate. Such unrequited <u>love</u> is a large part of the story of the Lord and His children. God creates the humans, supplies them with every good gift, bestows upon them honor and delight, teaches them the ways of blessing, rescues them from bondage and danger, accepts their pleas for pardon, does not give up on them. The Lord is "*steadfast and merciful, abounding in love and goodness.*" Yet, by word and deed, His children do not say "we love you, too." Just as your heart aches for a parent whose child does not love them, so we perhaps get a feel for the pathos of the Lord.

This plight of the lovelorn God is what Isaiah and the prophets dealt with and wrote about for centuries. The words in Isaiah 65 give us a feel for the hurting Father:

I stretched out my hands all day long to stubborn people. They chose to go the wrong direction. They followed their own plans. They constantly and openly provoked me.

This compassionate Creator is not the God many people seem to picture. Many folks evidently have in mind a cold and distant God, or a mean and vengeful God, or an impotent and irrelevant God. So long as those images dominate how people see their Maker, there will be no love lost toward Him. His love will then remain unrequited.

It was Isaiah more than any Older Testament prophet who foresaw the day when the Lord would take a new and decisive action to change the course of events. Isaiah was given a glorious glimpse of a Messiah to come. How far would God go to alter the death-bent direction of His beloved creatures? He would come in flesh Himself, show His face, and pour out His love even unto death! God cannot force you to love Him back. But when you do, there's a smile on His face — and on yours.

Notes

31
IsN'T LEVITICUS OBSOLETE?

*"Say to all the congregation of the people of Israel,
You shall be holy; for I the Lord your God am holy."*
— Leviticus 19:2

You may be familiar with the book of Leviticus. It is mostly all rules — ancient Jewish rules. Having been liberated from slavery in Egypt, and on the way to the Promised Land, the Lord gives Moses this book of laws on how to be a holy people for Him. God does not want His chosen people to just blend in and be like the pagan peoples all around them. So He not only gives them His love and blessings, He gives them laws for the living of their lives. Some of these are moral, some are civil, some are ceremonial. Some of these strike the modern ear as odd and even outrageous. Folks who want to blast and demean the Bible love Leviticus, since it contains some dietary laws and clothing laws and harsh punishments that they can ridicule in hopes of painting the whole Bible as irrelevant. We Christians have not prescribed many of these laws for 2,000 years now. They were needed for Moses and the ancient Israelites, but in Christ some of them are not now in force.

Nonetheless, we gladly keep Leviticus for its solid moral teachings and as a reminder that we in our time also are to be "*holy.*" That means: "set apart for God," "special," "different." The laws of God, the "shoulds" of our living and loving, still instruct and shape us. It works kinda like this.

Picture three pots of boiling water. Into one a carrot is dropped in. Into one an egg is dropped in. Into one a tea bag is dropped in. And the results are what? The same water that softens the carrot also hardens the egg. The Word of God brings softening to some, and it hardens others. Some people read *God's laws* — in Leviticus and elsewhere — and are moved to repentance and change. Others are repulsed. The Bible says that some have their hearts hardened. And what about the tea bag? When it is dropped in boiling water, it gives itself away and becomes the agent of change, not just the object that is changed. The water becomes tea! As we submit to the Lord and live out His Way, we are used by God to have a powerful effect on the world around us. That is what a holy people do.

Notes

32
Does God Hide From Us?

"Thou hast said 'Seek ye my face.' My heart says to thee 'Thy face, Lord, do I seek. Hide not thy face from me.'"

— Psalm 27:8

As a kid "hide and seek" was such a hoot — one of our most favorite games. Whether you were the hider or the seeker, it was fun. Even now as a grandpa I love it. It is a pure joy. You may notice that hide and seek are both mentioned in Psalm 27. (And these terms are sprinkled throughout the Scriptures; sometimes with the Lord God as the hidden one, sometimes as the Shepherd who seeks the lost. Ditto for the humans: sometimes they seek God and sometimes they hide from God.) In Psalm 27:8, the Lord says, "*Seek my face.*" And David pleads, "*Do not hide your face from me.*"

So does God hide a bit? Does He make us search? Is it part of the journey of faith to not always see God clearly? When the way is cloudy and the Lord is not as clear as day... when there is growing to do on our part...when there are lessons to be learned....the Father bids us "*seek my face.*" Is it like with our muscles, that only by some straining are they built up? Are there special joys hiding for those who trek the path of Christ? Jesus said to His first students: "...*seek and you shall find, knock and the door shall be opened to you*" (Matthew 7:7). Clearly the Christian way is not sedentary nor static. There is movement and change. There are obstacles and challenges. We never have it all figured out. Indeed, St. Paul says that, "*Now we see dimly, as in a mirror*" (1 Corinthians 13:12). By our daily life of faith, and over the years of our venture from cradle to grave, our Christ is in relationship with us. It's not a game, but the Father is enjoying us and developing us. Whether you are feeling as close to God today as if you were sitting on His lap, or perhaps you are really wondering "where on earth are you, Lord?" with David and many saints of old, we know that God has not gone away. Sometimes we seek a *hidden God*, but not a gone God.

    A little adage puts it this way: "On the cloudiest day of your life, the sun is still shining." David put it this way: "*I believe that I shall see the goodness of the Lord.*" So he reminds himself, and us: "*Wait with hope for the Lord. Be strong and let your heart be courageous.*" You'll see.

Notes

33

IS GOD REALLY WITH US?

> *"The angel of the LORD appeared to Gideon and said to him 'the LORD is with you, you mighty man of valor.' And Gideon said to him, 'Pray, sir, if the LORD is with us, why then has all this befallen us?'"*
> — Judges 6:12-13

I'll spare you any happy-talk about how great and blessed your days will all be. Some days — dare I say even some years — just plain are not peaceful and prosperous. It flat out isn't true that "everything will be fine." Our earthly days can be tedious and even rather torturous. When your shoulders sag under your load of troubles and your eyes wash over in tears, it is completely reasonable to ask, "Is God really with us? Has the Lord gone AWOL?" You can sure understand why some people <u>doubt</u> and despair about God and His goodness.

Even a biblical saint like Gideon had doubts. Midian, Israel's neighbor nation, had been ravaging Israel's towns and people for seven years. Their raiders looted and burned and killed with impunity. So when an angel told Gideon, *"the LORD is with you, mighty warrior,"* Gideon was skeptical. I appreciate the honesty of Gideon: *"...if the LORD is with us, why has all this happened to us?"* Uh huh. We get it. When it

– 68 –

sure looks to the obvious eye that God has abandoned you, how does someone have the nerve to say "*the* L ORD *is with you*"?

When our Christian maturity kicks in, we may be able to say (with stiff upper lip) that God's blessings are not synonymous with outward earthly delights. His inner spiritual gifts can also reveal His presence. But dog-gone-it, we need to see some practical blessings too, eh. God's goodness can't be just ideas and feelings, can't be all "someday by and by", right? Gideon did get to see real rescue and better days, though it took a long time. Israel did not become Utopia, but faith and joy can flourish when blessings are realized on earth. We need some real world evidence of God's lovingkindness. So…. hang in there…. And pray and work for those better days ahead. You don't have to be a mighty warrior, but you can be an instrument through whom the Lord accomplishes good things. Meanwhile, know that God won't bail.

Notes

34
How Is It That God Cares For Us?

"The LORD is my Shepherd, I shall not want."
— Psalm 23:1

Wouldn't you guess that the most well-known and well-loved chapter in the whole Bible is Psalm 23? It's comfort and beauty are so exceptional that we may at times gloss over the specifics of its content. The poetry is timeless; but its teaching is also timely. Even after 3,000 years, how we need the strong care that it lauds. It's a life-giving, lifetime security gift to have a personal shepherd.

Most of us have never seen an actual shepherd on duty. Sheep today in the U.S.A. are fenced in and fed, and a vet is just a phone call away. There is no personal, hands-on, 1:1 sheep-care. (Some might perceive today's human-care similarly: that we are fenced-in and fed, but impersonally managed. We have good supplies of food and clothing and shelter, yet many people are lost and lonely.)

Let's dissect the 23rd Psalm a bit, and focus on seven verbs telling us of what the Good Shepherd does. Much we need His tender care!

1. He "*makes me lie down in green pastures.*" He makes me. We often scurry about in futile pursuits; and the Lord says, "Hold up, rest your soul, enjoy the nourishment."
2. He "*leads me*" and "*He guides me.*" Though we Americans treasure our independence, I think we also see the essential need for good leadership. Some divine guidance would sure help these days. Some say that we are making excellent time, but don't know where we are going.
3. "*He restores my soul.*" Our storehouse of energy and goodwill get depleted regularly. We could use a refill in the spirit, and God's store is always open. When your reserves of peace or hope or compassion run low, the Shepherd can restore the soul.
4. "*You are with me.*" The Almighty is not aloof. He is Emmanuel: "*God with us*"; our dearest companion. Friends and family may come and go, or be absent a while; the Lord is ever near.
5. "*You comfort me.*" We sometimes get attacked and injured. When life leaves us hurting, we need a "fort" / a "fortress" / a haven for recovery. Where else can we turn when we've been battered about?
6. "*You prepare a table before me.*" God plans ahead / is prepared / is getting the banquet table all set — for you! Though our earthly eyes cannot see the heavenly mansion, we _trust_ God's promise.
7. "*You anoint my head with oil.*" The immutable ointment of the Lord's Name and love have been placed upon our heads, and we are sealed as His forever. We are marked with the cross of Christ for all eternity.

The Shepherd is on duty, today. He's got these good things at work, for you. We are in good hands.

35
WHY IS THE BIBLE CRITICAL OF US?

"Its heads give judgment for a bribe, its priests teach for hire, its prophets divine for money; yet they lean upon the Lord and say "is not the LORD in the midst of us? No evil shall come upon us."
— Micah 3:11

I hope you are feeling well and are in a good mood as you read this. That would increase the odds of your being able to handle some criticism. If criticism catches a person at the wrong time, it just cannot get through. And there are some times that it needs to get through. The prophet Micah — and most of the prophets — delivered a difficult message to God's people. They were not "yes-men" for the natural desires of the masses. They delivered the hard cold truth. Whether the criticism got through the defense shields that we humans use to filter out calls for change, I do not know. Micah sure tried.

He tells the people: "Here's the deal. The nation is way off track; the Lord is seriously ticked off at us, justifiably, and if we do not repent and change our ways, calamity shall befall us." Read Micah — or Amos or Zephaniah or most any of the "minor prophets" — and you'll get your ears singed. These books are where the "fire and brimstone" concept comes from. The people are being told "change your ways or you're gonna get it." And such a message is part of our Christian Bible. It's not our favorite part, nor the main part — "thank you, Lord!" — but it's kept there for our benefit. We prefer "chicken soup for the soul," but the Bible includes "red hot chili peppers for the soul." It's got plenty of criticism of our race. If you need constant affirmation, it's not for you.

In those minor prophet years, as in ours, people and nations sometimes get so blindly self-absorbed that we need a "don't make me come down there" call. Micah wrote about indulgence and violence and injustice and phoney-baloney religiosity. Does that shoe still fit? Do we also live too "high on the hog," and do we ignore the needy and abet wickedness? Do we get complacent in our religious routines? Well…. God Almighty has something to say about that. Don't rest easy. Humble yourselves before the Lord and seek His mercy and His *justice*. God is eager to forgive and to bring a brighter future.

Notes

36

IF WE KNOW HIM, WILL WE LOVE HIM?

"May the God of our Lord Jesus Christ, the Father of glory, give you a spirit of wisdom and of revelation in the knowledge of Him."
— Ephesians 1:17

Most people don't like the idea of having a king. Many people might love to be the king, calling all the shots. That'd be a massive ego boost, and such power, to be the king. But to have a king, not be the king, means that you clearly are not numero uno. If there is a king, and you're not it, that means you are a subject. You'd be not only not in charge, you wouldn't even be equals. You may be granted voice, but not vote. Sounds rather distasteful, eh? We don't like being told what to do! Indeed, America was founded purposefully to be anti-king. Democracy was / is our thing. We are very intentionally against monarchy. The world surely wouldn't like our "Christ the King" concept. Do we like it?

First, consider this: if there has to be a king, you'd want to at least be related to him. That you could stomach. Being a son or daughter of the king could be good, eh? You'd have perks; the smile of the sovereign would be upon you. You'd have a key to the palace. You'd be in proximity to the throne, and in the will! That'd all be good. But would it be enough?

So next, consider another step. To quell dissatisfaction with being an underling, and to prevent possible coup attempts, the king would have to be genuinely exceptionally good. To the power of the throne, kindness would have to be added. The king would have to win your heart. If the king were also your loving father, full of steadfast love and kindness, then there might be peace in the Kingdom.

Christian, that's your reality! By the Spirit's "*wisdom and revelation, you may know him better.*" Joy in the Lord, and happiness in serving Him, comes when we know Him better. To know Him is to love Him. The more you understand, the more you _praise_. Our king is worthy of all glory, laud and honor. Take the time to get acquainted. Think often about who He is. You might get started at this with some simple ABC's. "O God, you are Almighty Benevolent Creator! Divine Eternal Father! Gracious Holy Immortal Jesus! King, Lord, Master!" Got the picture? 'Tis wonderful to have Christ the King!

Notes

37
WHY SHOULD I BE THANKFUL?

"Have no anxiety about anything, but in everything by prayer and supplication with thanksgiving let your requests be made known to God."
— Philippians 4:6

How good it is. How good it is to gather together in the Name, and in the presence, of the Lord God of Love! It is His goodness, and our gratitude, that brings us together on days like Thanksgiving, and in fact every Sunday. As I think you know, the Lord is good. His generosity never runs dry; His blessings never cease; and His lovingkindness is eternal. God's goodness never fails. However, our gratitude sometimes falters. Our appreciation is intermittent. Our thankfulness blows hot and cold. Even in us, the family of God, who have drunk deeply of His mercy — our gratitude sometimes falters. Why is that? What can we do about that? How can our hearts and lives be more fully unleashed to glory in the Lord? Let's explore that a bit.

First, try reminding yourself of God's goodness. Your blessings come to you in two major categories: physical and spiritual. We get drenched by both in the Father's love. The physical blessings are those of the body, of nature, of material, of time, of things external. Go ahead and make a mental list of some of these (e.g. you can see, creation is incredibly beautiful and bountiful, you have food to eat, you are given a good number of years, etc.). God is good, and we are blessed physically. Then do the same with the spiritual realities. Yours today are love and hope and forgiveness and other internal gifts. Because you have Jesus, the Lord imparts His spiritual riches: peace of mind, purpose of days, joy of life, wellspring of love, intimacy with the Father, assurance of heaven, etc. God is good, and we are blessed spiritually.

Second, about that matter of our faltering gratitude. Though we'd like to have more grateful thanksgiving day by day, it seems to disappear more than we'd like. Could the problem be some blockage in our relationship with the Lord? We have this human habit of picking up and carrying around loads that we were not meant to bear. When you are weighed down, as if your backpack is full of bricks, the journey is hard and your gratitude is grounded. Some folks carry a sack of worry, internally fretting about all manner of things. They have not "*cast their burdens upon the Lord, knowing that He cares for you.*" The Lord is good, and He shall see you through. Along with the troubles of life, our Christ walks with us and enables us to know and _worship_ Him. Anxiety only blocks the way. St. Paul in Philippians 4:6 bids us to let our requests be made known, to go ahead and name them to God, and to do so with thanksgiving. That is, even before we see the light at the end of the tunnel, thank the Lord in advance that He will provide and He will prevail.

Gratitude is not just a gift for those who have things going their way. It is a gift for all of us in Christ, who know the eternal goodness of God.

Notes

38
WAS JESUS A SPELUNKER?

"When the time had fully come, God sent forth his son, born of woman, born under the law, to redeem those who were under the law, so that we might receive adoption as sons."
— Galatians 4:4-5

"Spelunking" is going into caves. A spelunker doesn't permanently live in a cave — like is said of some hermits — but he dares go in to explore and accomplish something and then come back out. Have you been in a cave? I have. I didn't like it much — too dark and dank. It's far superior to be out in the light and fresh air.

Caves are mentioned a little in the Good Book (including a kinda humorous story of David and Saul in 1 Samuel 24). Some think that Jesus' tomb near Jerusalem was probably a cave. Think now of a cave as a metaphor for earth. Not to say that earth is like a grim gray grave, but in contrast to Gloryland... you get it. From the brightness and sweetness of heaven above —- from the eternal perfect bond of His Father's side — <u>Jesus</u> came down to earth. He dropped way down, from the heights of glory, to enter our human darkness, all the way to the lowest of all low and lifeless spots: a shameful torturous execution. He brought His bright light into our dark cave. He knew we were trapped in sin and sorrow, with no way out. He came and said, "*Follow me; I know the way; indeed I am the way.*" He came to take us out of the shadowy life of the cave and usher us into eternal light.

Many choose to disregard His offer — and instead wander about looking for their own way, stumbling and groping along in the darkness. Strangely, some cave-dwellers think that it's not really so bad down below. They've gotten used to it, I guess. They've settled for the dim life: the division and violence and injustice and tedium. They may have given up all hope of anything better, ever. Their eyes have gotten adjusted to the dark. After all that cave-time, imagine how amazed they'd be to come up and see where Jesus leads! Picture the verdant hills, the sparkling waters, the gorgeous rainbow, the bounding children. Who'd want that cave?

Notes

39

WHERE CAN A PERSON FIND GOD?

"Therefore the Lord himself will give you a sign. Look, the virgin is with child, and shall bear a son, and you shall call his name Emmanuel."
— Isaiah 7:14

To find your way, some help is often needed. Be it cars on the road or visitors in a building — clear and visible signs are a must. For us church folks, we know that when you enter a church building you're not familiar with, it's very helpful to see well-marked signs pointing you to the office or sanctuary or bathroom. A good sign is a good sign that a church is newcomer-friendly.

If someone is a newcomer to the whole idea of God, and not familiar with the faith arena, where can they find God? What might help them to travel toward the Lord? If they were looking for assistance, what would do the trick? What *evidence* is there for God? Here are a few signs that might point in a beneficial direction.

Might a person find God in *nature*? Would creation be a compelling sign that there is a Creator? Behold, the stars and seas, the majesty and intricacy of the universe, the flowers that bloom and the birds that sing! Clear enough?

Perhaps such a sign works for some. I sure am awestruck by the world God has made. Yet some just don't seem to notice that nature is greater than just "natural." So some might need a clearer sign from God.

Would a lifetime of *gifts and goodness* be convincing? If you were freely given health and family and friends and talents and opportunities and second chances — without having to even ask — would that signal to you that you have a lavish and benevolent Maker? That'd do it for some. Others would attribute it all to chance.

Would the wisdom and truth of the totally unique *Holy Book* made of 66 books, that's been read and loved for 2,000 years and is still in daily use on all seven continents, would that be sufficient? If you knew the incredible interconnections of the Bible, and understood its variety and depth, its lasting universality, would you see in it the voice of God? Some would.

How about a *miracle* or two, done for your blessing? Would an amazing act of power or grace, that showered your life with delight or relief, and "came out of nowhere," would that trigger a committed faith? Well.... maybe.... for some.

Wait; there's more. The Lord Almighty upped His game to give the clearest possible revelation of Himself. At Christmas He came Himself! He came in the flesh, face-to-face, saying "here I am." That God would be born, incarnate, to walk and dwell among us, was the ultimate sign. You wanna see God?... know what He's like?.... what He thinks of you?.... what He wants of you? Well, here ya go: look at Jesus. Behold! This sign says "I love you. I give myself for you. I hold back nothing. I come naked and vulnerable. I will stop at nothing to win your heart." The cradle of Christ is where to find God.

Notes

40
WHY IS CHRISTMAS SUCH A BIG DEAL?

"In many and various ways God spoke of old to our fathers by the prophets; but in these last days he has spoken to us by a Son, whom he appointed the heir of all things, through whom also he created the world."
— Hebrews 1:1-2

There's no happier day on earth than Christmas. Now, it's true that all the festivities are not really Jesus-centric. We must admit that plenty of the happy happenings are about "Xmas" or "the holidays"; that the smiles are elicited by the material gifts or the cute children or the cherry pie. That's true. But let's not be killjoys to a season of earthly delights. Let's be big-hearted enough to let the joy of Christmas spill over onto those who have nary a thought of the Babe of Bethlehem. Grant them some good times. Yet, for those of us who love Jesus, and for those who are open to elevate their vision higher than those delectable Christmas cookies, let's ponder why Jesus is such a big fuss. What's the reason for this humongous season?

Hebrews 1:1-4 is one place that spells it out. Indeed, the whole book of Hebrews is one long sermon on Jesus. The author focuses on the identity of <u>*Jesus,*</u> and makes the repeated case that the Man from Nazareth is incomparable.

— 82 —

The key word for this book of the Bible is "superior." Jesus is compared to prophets, to angels, to priests, to Moses... and is determined to be superior to any and all of those. We're clear on His total uniqueness, yes? Though some ecumenists want to demote Jesus to just one member of the world's pantheon, and many secularists label Him a myth, or just another old dead white guy, don't fall for such a flattening of Christ and thereby of us all. Jesus is the Name above all names, the one and only Savior of our fallen human race. He alone is Lord. He alone is our hope. He alone is superior.

Hebrews 1:1-4 tells us why:

In many and various ways God spoke of old to our fathers by the prophets; but in these last days he has spoken to us by a Son; whom he appointed the heir of all things, through whom also he created the world.

God has spoken through prophets, yes. Indeed, that is the meaning of "prophet": one who speaks for God. There have been some great prophets, inspired with wisdom and courage to teach us humans about justice and kindness, about getting along and flying right. Be it biblical prophets like Isaiah and Amos, or current exemplary purveyors of the truths consistent with God's Word.... Yes, there are prophets. We're glad to have them. Bookstores have shelves full of their wisdom. However, though we honor prophets highly, they do not meet our greatest need. More than we need teaching, we need saving! More than we need a prophet, we need a Savior.

He is supernal ("heavenly; superlatively good") and eternal ("without beginning or ending"). So Christmas is not the birthday of a great guy. It is the entry into the world of the One who saves the world!

Notes

41

HOW DOES GOD CALL SOMEONE?

"And the Lord came and stood forth, calling as at other times, 'Samuel! Samuel!' And Samuel said 'Speak, for thy servant is listening.'"
— 1 Samuel 3:10

Let's say that there's a problem needing to be taken care of. Let's say that God has a task on earth that needs doing. Who will step up? It may be a heavy lift, or instead just an everyday matter. Who will do it? Many people could do it, many people see that it should be done — but who will? Fact is: lots of folks hesitate. It could be like in this quote by P. J. O'Rourke: "Everybody wants to save the world; nobody wants to help mom do the dishes." Uh huh.

Part of the story of our book, the Bible, is the recounting of individuals and groups who stepped up and helped accomplish the Lord's agenda. There are individuals like Noah, Moses, Esther and Paul. There are groups like the Israelites, the disciples and the church. In event after event, in both the older and newer Testaments, God uses people to take action for Him. Life is both individual and communal. You are part of a family and a church and a community; and at the same time you are your own person. Nobody else can be you. The Lord requires more than just an anonymous "somebody" — as in "somebody ought to do something about that."

That's how it worked for Samuel. Though only a boy, the Lord called him to step up. It's been said that when God wants something done, he chooses one person. In this Bible portion, the Lord needed to do something new and big for His wayward nation. He needed someone to step up and be His voice for that time. There was a ton of trouble in the land. God first chose one person: Samuel. God didn't select a committee. Similarly, God chose one person: Abraham, when He began a nation. He chose one person, Moses, when he worked Israel's deliverance from slavery. He chose one person, David, to slay the giant Goliath. He chose one person, Esther, to halt a holocaust. God chose one. One person individually can do mighty things in the service of the Lord.

The Lord called Samuel multiple times. Samuel didn't get it at first. It sure is nice to know that God grants second chances. And more. God keeps calling. So might there be something for you where you keep feeling "nudged" by the Spirit to step up and respond? Be it going across the street to meet a neighbor, or helping with 4th grade Sunday School, or speaking up about an injustice, or going on a mission trip, or.... it could be that you are the one that Christ is calling. You are somebody. _God calls_ people like you.

If you still feel uncalled and hesitant, God might even yet provide a helper for you. In Samuel's calling, an experienced "mentor" was needed to discern what was happening. When Samuel was confused and not getting it, he had an ally in Eli. Likewise, I bet you have some good experienced Christian in your life who can help you to hear the call. It could be your pastor, or even your grandma, but the Lord provides assistance. We don't need to just brush off our callings and thus miss our opportunities. Talk it over with a trusted and faith-filled friend. Pray about it with them. Ask God for ears to hear. Somebody gets the chance to step up.

42

WHAT IS THE 'KINGDOM OF GOD'?

[Jesus came preaching the gospel of God]... "saying, 'the time is fulfilled, and the Kingdom of God is at hand; repent, and believe in the gospel.'"
— Mark 1:15

We church-folk are used to hearing about *"the kingdom of God."* Perhaps it now seems mundane and tame. Perhaps we have domesticated this wild and radical vision. But be careful: it could break free and go on a tear at any time! Jesus called His entry into the world and His movement among humanity *"the kingdom of God."* His presence and His Way ushered in a whole new mode of living. In Him, God would reign, would re-do how we exist. In great contrast to our normal kings and kingdoms, the power of King Jesus is exemplified not in a sword, but in a cross. He rules not be force, but by service. He resides not in a palace in royal robes, but as a street person in common garb. He says a little child is great. He hangs out with hookers and money-grubbers. He takes on the lowly job of washing feet. He lives simply, turns the other cheek and forgives His enemies. He takes the path of service and love all the way to His own execution. Radical this is! He's not like other kings. This outrageous "kingdom of God" — also called "the kingdom of love" — totally redefines life.

The difference is "lion power" vs. "lamb power." Lion power dominates, and rules by fear. Lion power growls and prowls, and controls by the threat of violence. That's how normal earthly kingdoms and governments operate. You must do what they say or they will crush you. Lion power is "power over." The Kingdom of God reverses this. It's a 180° turn. With Lamb power the goodness of the Lord, not the might of force, calls the tune. This King has "power under," by coming up underneath us to forgive and to serve and to bless. Lamb power stoops to conquer by sacrifice. It's not a mere rotating of which person or party or program now gets to coerce you. The _kingdom of God_, with King Jesus, is love and grace divine.

In Mark 1, Jesus initiates this unlikely kingdom by calling disciples (that is, "trainees"). Mentioned there are common working men Peter and Andrew, James and John. They were not elite, not the sort of educated and privileged types most kings would covet. Two others who were called were Matthew (a traitor to Jews as a tax-collector for Rome), and Simon the Zealot (a sworn enemy of Rome). These two were far right-wing and far left-wing. Zealots sometimes assassinated tax-collectors! And yet, now with King Jesus, each has a transforming highest allegiance, that puts love and service above all. Somehow Jesus united these enemies and called each of them His friends, and put them to Kingdom use. My. He keeps doing it. He takes us, with our various types and stripes, and puts us in His service. In Him, we are one, despite our differences of gender or class or race or politics or age. For us all, He reigns by grace.

Notes

43

IS GOD USUALLY INCOGNITO?

"And after six days Jesus took with him Peter and James and John, and led them up a high mountain apart by themselves; and he was transfigured before them."
— Mark 9:2

Squint. Go ahead, there where you're sitting: squint your eyes such that most of the light is gone. (Pause.) With a good squint it's almost gray; you can see a little, but not nearly satisfactorily. Now, open those peepers up full and look around. Fantastic, eh! Glorious and bright is full vision. It's clear now, what you're looking at. The un-squint moves you from a tolerable but unfulfilled view, to the joy of blessed clarity. How majorly wonderful it is to have the gift of full and clear sight.

Transfiguration was the brilliant full exposure of Jesus. The "veil" of His humanity was pulled back and the disciples got a glimpse of His glory. In His earthly days, Jesus was sorta incognito. When people saw Him walking the paths of Galilee or fishing with His buddies or munching on olives, He looked just like any other Jewish guy. He didn't wander about with a shiny halo or a luminous aura. Not to say that He was "Clark Kent"... like Superman in disguise.... but

– 88 –

kinda like that. Now of course, correct Christian theology knows that Jesus was fully human, not just pretending to be one of us. Got it. His humanity was not a ruse, but His divinity wasn't obvious. Except on Transfiguration, and on Easter, when it was. That's our beautiful Savior shining on and illuminating the world. 2 Corinthians 3:18 says that "*we contemplate the Lord's glory.*" The glory of the Lord is sparkling / majestic / spectacular! Someday, friends in Christ, it shall be face to face. There shall be no veil, no squint, all glory. As the moving worship song puts it: "we can only imagine." Someday, we will fall on our knees and be spellbound. He will be totally awe-some!

Some skeptics, in fairness, just can't see it. They don't easily buy this perfect revelation of Jesus' true identity. We get their doubt. We admit: we weren't there, at either occasion: the transfiguration nor Easter. So….if we receive no physical / literal / earthly "ah ha" moment of full vision… on what do we base our faith? From where is our confidence? The person needing total proof most probably won't get it. The Almighty doesn't often force Himself on people in blazing glory. (Though of course there was that conversion of Saul to Paul thing, in dazzling, uninvited light.) It seems that most of the time God asks us for a bit of _faith_; says "trust me" even when its kinda squinty. Now, this is not "blind faith," as if God grants us nothing but unsubstantiated promises in the midst of our darkness. Oh no. His glory is there to be seen in the daily spectacle of nature, in miraculous moments like childbirth or rescue or healing or reconciliation, in the flash of insight or the realization of overwhelming mercy. The glory of God peeks through.

Notes

44
Who's Got The Holy Spirit?

"And suddenly a sound came from heaven like the rush of a mighty wind, it filled all the house where they were sitting. And there appeared to them tongues as of fire, distributing and resting on each of them."
— Acts 2:2-3

Lutherans are majorly different than Pentecostals. The stylistic difference is night and day. Lutherans are proper and quiet; we sing hymns and maybe chant Psalms; we follow the historic liturgy and lectionary; we are sacramental; we are non-emotional (rather stoic even). Pentecostals are pretty much the opposite. They are rambunctious; they may hoot 'n holler; they sway and raise hands; etc. Their lively style of worship would feel foreign to our mostly northern-European Lutheran sensibilities. Not many Lutherans would switch to Pentecostal, nor vice versa.

Dare I say that, theologically, we're not nearly so far apart? Lutherans and Pentecostals are both Protestant Christians. That means we both share the historic and orthodox tenets of the one holy apostolic Church. The central dogmas of belief are identical: the triune God, the sinful humanity, the savior Jesus, the holy Bible, the love of the Church, the assurance of heaven. We are brothers and sisters in Christ. We may look askance at each other even so. They may think that we "*quench the Spirit,*" omit the "*gifts of the Spirit,*" are not "*filled with the Spirit.*" We may think they require a showiness of the Holy Spirit that is not necessary. They sometimes demand a speaking in tongues. Martin Luther said they "swallowed the Holy Spirit, feathers and all."

On the Day of Pentecost, all Christians are "pentecostal." As the Holy Spirit was powerfully and vividly poured out upon the believers, to jump-start the Church and send forth the Gospel, it's a holy and happy day for us all. Without the mighty wind and the tongues of fire and the passionate preaching about Jesus, this Christian-thing would be a minor footnote in history. We had to have Pentecost! The Trinitarian truth is that God as Creator and Savior was not enough. God on high and God on the cross also needed God on the move. We believe in and adore and need Father, Son and Holy Spirit.(A 3-legged stool works; a 2-legged stool does not.)

The Spirit comes again today to do the animating work our hearts need. The Spirit convicts us of sin, comforts us in sorrow, illuminates Christ, counsels us with divine guidance, and kindles in us a zeal for the Lord. Do we Lutherans need that? Ubetcha! (Or a silent nod of Amen, if that's more comfortable.) Lutherans may not be Pentecostals, but Lutherans, too, do Pentecost. With Christians everywhere we pray, "Come Holy Spirit; light our hearts afire."

Notes

45
WHAT'S WITH THE TRINITY-THING?

"This Jesus God raised up, and of that we are all witnesses. Being therefore exalted at the right hand of God, and having received from the Father the Promise of the Holy Spirit, he has poured out this which you see and hear."
— Acts 2:32-33

Much as we worship and adore our 3-in-1 God, we can't fully explain Trinity. How is it that God is Father, Son and Holy Ghost; but yet the Lord is one God, not three? Well…. Shall I take a swing at it? We know that Trinity is a *description* not an *explanation*, but we sure want to try to grasp how this can be. So, though this could be just another swing and a miss, I hope we believers maybe will on occasion get at least a foul-tip… a swing and a piece-of-it.

Pastor Tim Keller in his book, *Reason For God*, uses the image of a *dance* for the Trinity. He pictures three distinct and beautiful beings interlocked in one moving, flowing dance. Together they glide, inseparably, bringing life and goodness. It is joy and love in motion. It is the dance of everlasting grace. Trinity as dance focuses on relationship. From eternity God is about relationship, not a solitary aloof Higher Power. That's helpful, and adorable too, eh?

In case that struck you as strike one in what is but another flailing away at *Trinity*, here I try again. My wife likes this one, although I imagine professional theologians may not. She thinks of God with different *hats*. To accomplish His love for the world, the Lord has a golden crown as King Eternal, and a crown of thorns as Redeemer of sinful humanity, and a flowing cap as Muse of inspiration. One great God, three distinct hats. The Lord cannot be the fullness of God if only Creator, or if only Crucified Christ, or if only Empowering Counselor. All three, in one, make God God. Hats. Hmmm... Nice try? Strike two?

I hope you can be OK with not totally understanding the Trinity-thing. God is so much higher and greater than us, that it makes sense that He is beyond our understanding. No insult intended, but as a dog sorta gets us humans but can't fully understand, so for us. The Eternal and Almighty Master of the Universe is beyond our full comprehension. Yet the Lord is not beyond our adoration for Who He is. With all believers again today, we shall thank and praise, serve and obey Father, Son and Holy Spirit.

Notes

46

DOES GOD PICK SIDES?

"If it had not been the Lord who was on our side, when men rose up against us..."
— Psalm 124:2

There are many things in the Bible that strike the 21st century mind as unpalatable. Those who study the sociology of religion have surveys and statistics to tell us that many Americans do not like certain biblical views. For those Christians who see the Scriptures as primarily a "Book of Faith" — i.e. *theology* — they can just set the troublesome ideas aside as "that's just what those ancient authors thought." They think we've "evolved." For us Christians who honor the Good Book as the Word of God — i.e. *Revelation* — we are left to figure out how best to accept and deal with difficulties. One such item appears here in Psalm 124, and repeatedly in holy writ: that the Lord sometimes gets directly involved for some people and against others. This is in stark contrast to the enlightenment mind, which prefers any deity to be neutral. It's not offensive to go with the Deist theology, that has God benevolent but aloof. But to say, like the Psalmist, that "*the Lord is on our side*" opens the door wide to a parochial patriotism that baptizes our team and our desires as "God is on our side." Abraham Lincoln is attributed with the more broad-minded quote: "Let's not worry whether God is on our side, but whether we are on God's side." Wise, eh? Dignified, too. Peaceable, also.

The problem is:

1. A distant, non-intervening, neutral God is not biblical. You might get a "Bible" you like better, but you have neutered the holy Word. You then just choose the parts that fit your supposedly superior personal view of things.
2. It leaves you with a God who's quite irrelevant to daily life and struggles. Such a Higher Power could be therapeutic and spiritual, but would clearly not be the _sovereign_ Lord God Almighty of the Bible.

The Lord was for Israel and against their enemies. He is for the righteous and against the wicked. This must not bleed over into jingoism, but neither can Christians accept an insipid and impotent "God." The Lord cares enough to take sides... always for good. Such a concept is very scary to the secularists, and to governments, since God is thus Judge of earth, not us.

(Now, I don't think that God takes sides in football, like pro-Vikings and anti-Packers... nor in lots of everyday life and politics... but He is not complacent about how important things turn out.)

Notes

47
Does God Spank?

"It is good for a man that he bear the yoke in his youth. Let him sit alone in silence when he has laid it on him."
— Lamentations 3:27-28

Perhaps I am sticking my feet in a steaming pile of doodoo with the above question. I shall not enter into the combustible topic of whether parents should spank their kids. (Well, maybe I'll just sorta step close.) Some parenting experts — especially those without kids — say, "No, never ever spank; it teaches violence." Other parenting experts say that as a rarely used tool in your toolbox, with a young child and no hostility, it can sometimes prove valuable. All parenting experts realize that children must have guidance and correction, or they shall surely be spoiled brats. Be it via a spank or a time-out, a stink-eye or logical consequences, parents properly shape their offspring. Do you remember how your parents disciplined you? Hopefully they did it well and you love them.

Related to our divine Parent now — our Father in heaven — does the Lord *discipline*? The Bible unequivocally says, "Yes!" God is kind, but not soft. He is not our grandfather who art in heaven, not a pushover papa. Any number of Scriptural references make this clear, like in Hebrews 12: "*The Lord disciplines him whom he loves, and chastises every son whom He receives.*" Lamentations 3 says likewise. Jeremiah, "the weeping prophet," knows too well the weight of God's hand upon Israel. He is experienced at "waiting quietly" and "bearing the yoke" and "sitting alone is silence when he has laid it on him" and "being in the dust." He tells us that "*though God cause grief... He does not willingly afflict the sons of men.*" Jeremiah laments his situation; even if it be from God. Jeremiah yet trusts "*the steadfast love of the Lord*" and proclaims that "*great is Thy faithfulness,*" even in proximity to suffering and discipline. Can we see it that God does not want us to be spoiled brats, and we might thank Him for it?

Jeremiah even praised God in the bad times. Does it seem incredulous that a person could extol God, even in the midst of correction? Can Christians worship and pray and stay faithful, even when they are receiving correction? Only, only if there is an established and overarching relationship of love. If we know that the Lord loves us and has blessed us and has our best long-term interest at heart, then even our hardships and hard lessons of life can be received as within the sovereignty of the Father. (Did I step in it?)

Notes

48

DOES GOD GET THWARTED?

"And Jesus could do no mighty work there, except that he laid his hands upon a few sick people and healed them."
— Mark 6:5

In the big picture, the idea that the Master of the universe could be thwarted would be inconceivable balderdash. "No way, no how" a devout Calvinist would say; holding that the <u>sovereign</u> Lord of all creation just cannot be stymied. "God's will is supreme, and neither creature nor creation can get in His omnipotent way" would be the firm position of many Christians. In the final tally, I fully agree. We who worship the Almighty Triune God know that He shall prevail. He shall have His way. Read all about it in Revelation.

However, it appears that sometimes — in the meantime, in our interim embattled status prior to the final curtain — not everything goes God's way. The Lord has granted some measure of free agency to His image-bearers, and we earthlings sure don't always do what God wants, eh. Plus, the Father's adversary the devil isn't yet gone, and he wreaks a lot of havoc on earth that is contrary to God's wishes. So dare I say that yes, God does not always get what He wants. His perfect will is for peace, but war exists; He desires unity, but we keep fracturing; His mandate is love, yet many are haters.

In Mark 6, Jesus gets a bit of a rebuff in his own hometown. The folks there take offense at him, and "*He could do no mighty work there.*" Their recalcitrant will gets in the way of His good will. Notice that even then Jesus heals some, and stays at his work, and empowers His disciples. Jesus is not defeated, but is held back a bit. He's got to detour. He's gonna win, but those blasted humans are making it difficult.

So don't be dismayed when you see things go clearly contrary to the goodness of Christ. The dark side will, alas, score some points and thwart the divine intent for a time. Earth is not heaven. That doesn't mean all is lost. Satan may win some battles, but he cannot win the war. We who are on Jesus' team will keep working and praying that God's "*will be done, on earth as it is in heaven.*"

Notes

49

DO YOU NEED A SIGN FROM GOD?

"I set my bow in the cloud, and it shall be a sign of the covenant between me and the earth."
— Genesis 9:13

We humans would sure like more clarity and less cloudiness about life. Instead of head-scratching uncertainty concerning God's will and our lives, why doesn't the Lord just spell it out in an unmistakable way? We'd like to have a sign from God. Why doesn't He communicate in more open and obvious ways? Couldn't He talk into our ear, or write letters in the sky, or work a miracle? We'd like <u>evidence</u>.

Well, sometimes He does that. The Bible reveals God's *"signs and wonders"* that tell us about His character and will. Think of the signs He gave Pharaoh to let His people go. Think of the manna from heaven that revealed His providence. Think of the many manifold miracles in Scripture that were loud and clear signs from God.

Genesis 9 is the follow-up on Noah and the flood, and it includes a sign from God: the rainbow. It is to stand as a sign of the Lord's promise for all generations. When people saw the bow in the clouds they were to remember that God is gracious, will send good things after any storm, and will not destroy the earth with a flood. Now, do people today see the rainbow as a sign from God? Hmmm... In recent decades, the rainbow sign has been taken over by the LGBT community as their sign. Only biblically literate Jews and Christians would know that it's a sign of God's mercy.

Devout believers see signs from God in every newborn baby, every sunrise, every starry night. Some Christians are keen to see God's signs in various events unfolding in their lives. Excellent. And every Christian sees the one main sign from God: the cross. Across the ages and around the world it says clearly that the Lord loves us to death, and that not even ugly execution can stop His everlasting love. It's a sign. It's loud and clear. Take a good long look there, and see what the message is from your loving Father.

Notes

50

DOES GOD END PEOPLE'S LIVES?

"For I have no pleasure in the death of anyone, says the LORD God; so turn and live."
— Ezekiel 18:32

You've heard it like at funerals and such: "The Lord called her home," or "God wanted her up with Him," or "Jesus needed another choir member." Hmmm... While it is totally true that the Lord God is sovereign and can run His universe however He wants, I'm a bit ambivalent on this question. (That's the same as wishy-washy, right?) Here's my conundrum: I know that God is good and is on the side of life, not death. *"Every good endowment and every perfect gift is from above"* (James 1:17). I also know our terrestrial viewpoint is limited, so that we are blocked from seeing the whole story. *"For my thoughts are not your thoughts, neither are my ways your ways, says the Lord"* (Isaiah 55:8).

I realize there is plenty of biblical evidence that God sometimes takes people out. (Ananias and Sapphira in Acts 5 to name just two.) Mix in the free-will factor: that we humans are the cause of many things, including many <u>deaths</u>. And don't forget Satan, God's adversary, who is out to "*steal and kill and destroy*" (John 10:10). Stir it all together and what'dya got? Muddlety?

Some Christians find great comfort in that "God is in control" and that "*not a sparrow falls to the ground*" apart from God's will. They'd rather have the Almighty Lord responsible for even death that to cede to cosmic chaos. They don't want life to have random luck as the cause of major things like death. Other Christians think that it's horrible to have God somehow linked to the grim reaper. They'd be inconsolably angry with a God who took away their loved one. They want the Father always fighting for the lives of His children. To put God together with the one deciding who lives and who dies is just unacceptable for some. I get that, don't you?

As I write this on a Good Friday, with Jesus' death definitely part of God's design for a higher good, I know that He beats death; and that He can use even death to accomplish eternal good. So, I rest in the confidence that the Lord will work things out; and I'll say, "Yes, at least sometimes God does end people's lives." (That may be both wishy-washy and hard to swallow.) Do you and your group have a good solution to this muddlety?

Notes

51

DOES SATAN ATTACK PEOPLE?

"Be sober, be watchful. Your adversary the devil prowls around like a roaring lion, seeking someone to devour."
— 1 Peter 5:8

Really?! This question is still posed in the 21st century? Hasn't the idea of "Satan" been harpooned and lampooned as an archaic vestige of pre-enlightenment thinking? I'm not sure what percentage of Americans believe in the devil, but it's likely low. Even many Christians have tossed him out with the boogeyman. A chunk of Western Christianity has reconstructed our faith and fired <u>Satan</u>. (As if they get to decide that.) Historic orthodox Christianity — based on the plain sense of Scripture — still deals with the devil. The Bible describes him as a fallen angel, God's Adversary, the father of lies, the prince of darkness, and the accuser of the faithful. Some of the language about him in the Good Book is figurative: as a serpent or a roaring lion, true. Yet the existence of an enemy of the Lord who is out to ruin everything and win the cosmic war vs God and His goodness is clearly biblical.

Most commonly, Satan works via stealth and deception. Generally he comes after us with tricks, tempting us into despair or arrogance or laziness or such mind-games. He wants to gently and unnoticeably coax you off the path of life. The way down is often gradual and reasonable. Like a marriage that slowly decays as the couple grows apart, so does our foe erode faith and obedience. It's slow-motion demonic.

However, sometimes the Dark One just directly assaults. He may inflict accident or illness or addiction as his weapons. He may "gut-punch" you and get you disoriented. You know the experience? I do. Some days you are in a total funk, a pit of darkness due to some travail, and you can't just calmly, rationally snap out of it. It's like your heart is broken, or a thick cloud fogs you in, or you're beside yourself with some fear or anger. Life is not merely reasonable. There are deep inner forces at work. It's satanic. Pray for the Lord to fight for you vs. the destructive powers. The foe is mighty, but remember: God is Almighty.

Notes

52
DOES GOD DITHER?

"Now Jesus loved Martha and her sister and Lazarus. So when he heard that he was ill, he stayed two days longer in the place where he was."
— John 11:5-6

If you were to list the Lord's attributes, your list might include "eternal," "compassionate," "omniscient," "generous," etc. The character of God is worthy of our contemplation. And would "patient" be on that list? We really appreciate the Lord's patience — most of the time. We love it that He delays judgement and bears with us and is willing to wait for our maturity. Patience is a great virtue. However, when it comes to answering our prayers and delivering His blessings, we'd like God to hurry up. We want the Lord to be patient with our failings, but not with our blessings. The heavenly Father is not in a hurry. He doesn't act hastily. But, my….. sometimes it's so hard to wait! Don't the faithful sometimes wonder, "What's taking Him so long? Why the delay? Is the Almighty dithering around up there while we are in distress?"

Think of Martha and Mary waiting anxiously for Jesus to show up as Lazarus lay dying. Jesus didn't rush in. He waited two days to show up. When He did arrive, Martha blurts out "*Lord, if you had been here, Lazarus wouldn't have died!*" We understand her frustration. Think of Jeremiah being asked to pray for Jerusalem's guidance, and "*ten days later the Word of the L*ORD *came to Jeremiah.*" (see Jeremiah 42). A ten-day wait might feel like a lifetime. Think of the poor soul who is ill, or broke, or lonely, and asks God for help... and yet there's a long delay. What's with that? Arrrghh.

We don't want to accuse the Lord of dithering, but it is obvious that His timing is not always to our liking. "*His ways are not always our ways.*" His plans may need time to unfold. His agenda sure does not always include our comfort. Drat. God has a lot more time than we do; and when He waits to act and answer, we try to trust that He's up to something very good. _Faith_ is that challenging inner confidence that the Father has not forgotten us and that He will come through for us. Though we hate to wait, the Lord loves to bless.

Will His patience bring about ours?

Notes

FAITH QUESTIONS

What's a Christian to do & does it make sense?

Ethics

53
WHY DOESN'T CHRISTIANITY WORK BETTER?

"And fear came upon every soul; and many wonders and signs were done by the apostles."
— Acts 2:43

    This Holy Christian Church on earth, that carries forward the life and love of Jesus, just feels weak and clunky so often. We are chosen of God, ordained for Gospel service in a thirsty world, and yet... so frequently we are not world-beaters. Perhaps we even feel world-beaten. Though we know the Truth: that God is great and good, that His love is eternal and triumphant, that Jesus is our perfect redeemer... yet... it's a slog. Life is hard. The <u>Church</u> struggles. We don't often seem to rise and shine for our King. We don't often seem to soar and score for the Lord. What's up with that?
    The biblical image is that we are "winded." We are out of breath. On our own, we just don't have the airflow capacity to do much. We may not be totally flat-lined and in need of direct CPR, but we are in dire need of resuscitation. We need the life-giving infusion of the Lord's mighty wind. Without the Holy Spirit's breath into us, the Church, we are somewhere between anemic and downright dead. We may

move about and go through some motions — zombies as it were — but we would lack all vim and vigor. You know that zombies are scary — religious zombies doubly so. To have empty bodies — soulless corpses — prowling about inflicting untold damage to God's creation, is a sight no one should see. It would be "*walking by the flesh*" in St. Paul's words; as opposed to "*walking by the Spirit.*" It would be like the Pharisees as "*white-washed tombs,*" in Jesus words.

Praise God, He has another option! The Lord has a better way! It need not be zombie existence for us! It was proven and demonstrated on the glorious day of Pentecost. Upon a group of disheartened but hopeful disciples, who knew the truth of Jesus' resurrection but were not yet empowered to do anything with that truth, the mighty wind blew. Going from empty to full, the Holy Spirit was poured out and the ragtag apprentices of Jesus became in fact world-beaters. Check it out by reading the second chapter of Acts. The Christ-followers blossomed and spread. Today, again, blow, Spirit, blow!

Notes

54
WHAT IF I DON'T FEEL LIKE WORSHIPPING?

"Ascribe to the Lord, O families of the peoples, ascribe to the Lord glory and strength!"
— Psalm 96:7

Is it harmful and repressive to disregard your feelings? Our culture and most counselors would probably say so. We modern liberated Americans are big into feelings. We want to express ourselves, and "get real" and "tell it like it is." We are told to "go with your heart" and to "listen to your gut." It might be considered dishonest and unhealthily stoic to suggest otherwise. Dare Christians offer a different take on this?

Instead of a life in bondage to myself, instead of a world that revolves around me and my response to what goes on in my sphere, the Lord invites us into something with a higher horizon and a bigger focus. Life for us on Earth is not to be about us. Christians are those who live in surrender to Christ. It's His world and I am just a bit player on His stage. God is God and I am not. I am here to do His bidding, not He mine. Some would say that such thinking squashes us. We Christians think it liberates us and lifts us.

We are freed up to know and love God, to worship the King of the universe, to partake in His large Life and Love, not just our little doings.

So when the Psalms, like Psalm 96, over and over bid us to "*sing,*" "*praise,*" "*announce,*" "*give,*" "*rejoice,*" etc. —the Lord is not asking us to feel a certain way. How we feel this morning has little to do with it. The great news of our mighty and merciful Lord comes to us not through our gut, nor even our eyes. It comes through the ear. We have gotten the Word: the unassailable and eternal Truth that God is great and God is good! He is our beginning and our end! He loves you, little mortal, and He has won for you blessings now and glory to come! So rejoice. He's got you. It is a gift to gather with others, and to build up community.

So yes, I am saying "go to church," whether you feel like it or not. Do the right thing and the Lord will be at work — even helping your feelings to come along to the right place. And if those feelings are quite sad and painful, you probably should talk with someone about that.

Notes

55

CAN GOD'S ENEMIES BECOME ALLIES?

"They heard it said: 'He who once persecuted us is now preaching the faith he once tried to destroy.'"
— Galatians 1:23

Try this, would you: picture in your mind the person you know who has the most strongly negative view of our faith. He or she would be most unlikely to set foot in church or offer a prayer or speak a good word for the Christ-followers. They would maybe blast Christians for being hypocrites or legalists or haters. The odds of their *conversion* would be slim and none. An autobiographical portion of Galatians illustrates that slim does not equal none.

There was no more committed an opponent of Jesus than Saul of Tarsus. He was a fanatic fundamentalist Jew who was having Christians arrested and even killed. (Check it out in Acts 6-9.) It took an act of God — it always does — but the one who hated and persecuted the church rather quickly became the chief apologist and greatest missionary in the history of Christendom. Fire-breathing Saul became Spirit-filled Paul. The Lord God wanted this man on His team and He went after him. The gifts and the zeal that Saul used against the church would be now used in superlative service to Jesus the Christ. (Not everyone knows that C.S Lewis, one of the greatest Christian writers of the 20th century, was once anti-faith also.)

Does this not fill your heart with hope? We believe, contrary to normal human experience, that people can really change! The hateful can become loving. Enemies can become friends. Cowards can become courageous. The spiritually dead can be resurrected and made new. If our Lord could do it to Saul, He can do it for the vilest sinner or the smuggest snob. Or even you. We Christians believe in redemption. Praise God, Jesus on the loose is the Hope of the world! Those aggressive anti-Christians might be yet used of the Lord.

So now picture that unbeliever again... and pray for them, for God to bless them and reach them and break through their defense shields. Paul tells us "*God wants all to be saved and to come to the knowledge of the truth*" (1 Timothy 2:4). He won't give up. You neither?

Notes

56

IS HEARTFELT FAITH KINDA EMBARRASSING?

"And standing behind Him at His feet, weeping, she began to wet His feet with her tears, and wiped them with the hair of her head, and kissed His feet, and anointed them with the ointment."
— Luke 7:38

Lots of people break bread with Jesus. Our Lord will come eat with anyone. There's sure good news in that. We see Him go to the house of traitorous tax-collectors in the Gospels, and now in Luke 7 He is at the table of a Pharisee. These were the buttoned-down, upstanding citizens of town. These were the successful leaders, who often exuded an aroma of snobbishness. They are kind of the "bad-guys" of the Gospels, so it is nice to see our Christ give them some personal time. They need Him too. However, at this banquet there appears to be a party-crasher. A woman of ill-repute has snuck in — she definitely would not have been invited — and rather makes a scene. She throws herself at Jesus in utter adoration. She is weeping and kissing and getting in Jesus' personal space. How embarrassing, eh. The Pharisees are not pleased that the good rabbi allows this public display of affection.

So Jesus makes it a teachable moment. Not so concerned with outward decorum and more interested in inward intention, our Wondrous One reveals a great truth: "*the one who is forgiven little loves little.*" The way you see yourself will shape the way you respond to Jesus. The Pharisees felt pretty good about themselves; they were comfortably self-righteous. They didn't need mercy; indeed they figured they were due affirmation. So there was no need to pour out adulation on this upstart teacher from Nazareth. The woman off the streets, on the other hand, brought a broken humility. She would not even pretend to be acceptable. She literally threw herself at Jesus' feet. Thus she was the one in position to be lifted up. She who was forgiven much, loved much. Hopefully, she could in turn forgive much and love much. So, you see the difference. Her awareness of her own sin results in her outpouring of <u>worship</u> to Jesus.

I am not suggesting that you make a scene on your way up to communion, but the Word of the Lord here teaches us that when the grace of Jesus has reached into the depths of our hearts it will open up a flow of love that cannot stay buttoned down. When the compassion of Christ touches our hearts, it results in passion for Him and love for others. A direct hit of the grace of God makes a huge difference.

Notes

57

CAN I BE A CHRISTIAN WITHOUT A CHURCH?

"Bear one another's burdens, and so fulfill the law of Christ."
— Galatians 6:2

What do you think: is being a Christian a solo activity, or a group activity? Are you a believer in Christ, or part of the Body of Christ? The correct answer is, "Yes"; you are both. No one can believe for you. No one can make you follow Jesus, and no one can do the following for you. True. It is also true that we are of great importance to the faith and faithfulness of others. We are in this together. We are not independent and on our own. We are brothers and sisters in the family of God. Neither independent from others nor dependent on others is best; but rather, interdependent. In the first verses of Galatians 6, you see what could look like a contradiction. Verse 2 says "*carry each other's burdens.*" Verse 5 says "*each one must carry his own load.*" Hmmm... Which is it?

Yes, it is both. Baseball is a good analogy. Is the team dependent on the individual, or is the individual dependent on the team? Both. To win, you have to work together and support each other. When one player has a bad day, others have to step up for the good of the team. It is also true that one player at a time steps into the batter's box and is "up to bat." The next guy may be "on deck," but he cannot hit for you. Both the individual and the team are necessary. Star players (and Christians) do not make a winning team; nor does the team (_church_) win without exemplary individuals. Can you be a baseball player and not be on a team? Can you be a soldier and not be in the army? Can you be a husband and never be at home? Well, maybe technically, but not with any effectiveness.

St. Paul is telling us that you are not "on your own" to sink or swim. You do not carry the whole weight of Jesus' ongoing Kingdom on your little shoulders. Yet, you are needed to do what the good Lord has enabled you to do. No one else can be you. You have unique abilities and opportunities; you have a circle of influence that no famous super-Christian can cover for you. And you have wonderful teammates to walk alongside and pull with you. God has provided us with each other, for mutual support. We can do so much more together than we can alone.

The Christian life is both alone and together. It's quite ingenious of God, isn't it?

Notes

58
CAN OUR FAITH BE STOLEN?

"See to it that no one makes a prey of you by philosophy and empty deceit, according to human tradition, according to the elemental spirits of the universe, and not according to Christ."
— Colossians 2:8

If you got robbed, you would notice, right? If it was something valuable taken from you, you would not fail to see it — unless it happened quite slowly and quietly. If the loss was more like erosion than outright larceny, it could go undetected. The amount of beautiful topsoil that America loses each year to erosion, done imperceptibly by wind and rain, is huge. The amount of cash and inventory that is taken each year in business, by embezzlement or cyber-stealing, is huge. It is slow robbery.

In Colossians 2:8, St. Paul says, "*Be careful not to let anyone rob you of the faith, through a shallow and misleading philosophy.*" He knew that <u>faith</u> can be stolen. He knew that there in Colossae, and also here, there are people and forces out to remove you from your union with Christ. Of course, the great thief is Satan, out to "*steal and kill and destroy,*" as Jesus explained (John 10:10). It's a very good thing we have a Good Shepherd to be the guardian of our

— 120 —

souls! To not "*fall prey*" to the devil and his minions of an increasingly aggressive secularism, Paul offers some security tips. In verses 6 and 7 of Colossians 2, he recommends:

1. "*Continue to live as Christ's people.*" This is like a neighborhood watch program: a buddy system, keeping an eye and a heart out for each other. The isolated Christian falls prey.
2. "*Sink your roots in Him.*" Grow some depth and maturity of faith. Be in the Word and in prayer daily, so that when drought days come you will withstand. Jesus told that great parable about the sower and the need for deep roots.
3. "*Build on Him.*" Put some effort into development; be a builder and encourager. Just as you do home maintenance or the place declines, build faithfully. Jesus said "*the wise man builds his house upon the rock.*"
4. "*Overflow with thanksgiving.*" A grateful heart stays strong. Count your blessings. Sing your praises. If a person or a congregation stops being thankful, and the eyes are not on the prize, there is vulnerability for faith-theft.

We too live in perilous times. It's no cinch that faith will be kept. Paul is helping us: forewarned is forearmed. Don't get robbed.

Notes

59
WERE THOSE BIBLE HEROES ALMOST PERFECT?

"Now faith is the assurance of things hoped for, the conviction of things not seen. For by it the men of old received divine approval."
— Hebrews 11:1-2

There are a lot of great chapters in the Bible: Genesis 1, Psalm 23, Isaiah 55, Luke 15, Philippians 4. A sure contestant for the "Top 10 Chapters of the Good Book" would be Hebrews 11. It is the "roll call of faith heroes." It gives a brief glimpse of Noah, Abraham, Jacob, Joseph, Moses, etc. It provides examples of people who trusted in the Lord, holding them up as models of faith. Although they made the "Hall of Fame" in biblical terms, you do know that these people were not stainless, right? Not to shock you, but Noah was a drunk, Jacob was a cheat, and Moses was a murderer. Abraham and Joseph were not nearly perfect either. Hmmm... So, you don't have to achieve moral perfection to be a faith-hero. Indeed, you cannot achieve moral _perfection_. We are all fools and sinners. "*None is perfect, no, not one*" is how Isaiah puts it.

So with that settled.... now what? Now we can start with today and proceed to trust in God as Hebrews 11 encourages us. Our merciful and mighty Lord gladly forgives, and patiently keeps offering us opportunities to step forward in faith! We get our chance, in our lifetime, to contribute to the work of the Lord on earth. Redeemed by grace, we are empowered to have a little faith and let the Lord use us.

Hebrews 11 begins by giving us a definition of faith: "*Faith is the assurance of the things hoped for and the conviction of things unseen.*" Faith is the confidence in God — not in yourself — to live out a trusting relationship with Him in the time and place you find yourself in. It is the Spirit-inspired courage to do what God asks of you. This is not a private little transaction that remains just inside you. It manifests itself in your real-life response to the Lord. The heroes of Hebrews 11 are not named because they had sweet intentions. It is not like that dreadful saying: "It's the thought that counts." That is one of the worst sayings ever. Faith is not a thought. It is letting God move in you and through you according to His will. You may not make the Hall of Faith, but know that our gracious God can and will do good things through you!

Notes

60
WHO KISSES IN CHURCH?

"Steadfast love and faithfulness will meet; righteousness and peace will kiss each other."
— Psalm 85:10

Kissing is allowed in church, but normally just during weddings. (Additionally, mothers kissing babies would be approved.) Kissing is not a common biblical topic, but it does show up in Scripture. We all know about Judas' "kiss of death" with which he betrayed Jesus. Of a much more salutary nature is the kiss we see in Psalm 85. There the kissers are not people, but rather are spiritual realities. "*Righteousness and peace kiss each other.*" (If you were hoping for a dish of romance or PDA, you are now disappointed.)

A kiss is a positive and intimate connection. A kiss links favorably. It's a sweet thing when a loved one gives you a kiss. The Psalmist is picturing for us the positive linkage of righteousness and peace. If you want righteousness (i.e. right behavior), it must be closely joined with peace (i.e. kindly goodwill). You will not get healthy moral lives without gentle graciousness. Righteousness and peace must

— 124 —

kiss. Have you heard the adage, "If you want peace, work for justice"? Martin Luther King Jr. said, "He whom you would change you must first love." A little girl once prayed "Lord, please make the bad people good, and the good people nice." Each of these makes connections between good things, as in: can't have one without the other. The will of the Lord comes about when both our actions and our hearts are joined. Outward behavior and inward disposition are linked. A healthy faith is wholistic. A sick faith is a bad thing; as someone has said, "Religion makes bad people worse." You get that: faulty religion can do a lot of harm. A sweet faith, of both inner and outer goodness, is life-giving.

Psalm 85:10 starts with, "*Love and faithfulness meet together.*" Out of a heart of goodwill, plus deeds that are faithful (virtuous), does God accomplish His holy desires for us. Pray for kissing: that our lives be wholistically connected as God woos and wins us, body and soul.

Notes

61

MUST CHRISTIANS SUBMIT?

"Be subject to one another out of reverence for Christ."
— Ephesians 5:21

"Submit" is not a four-letter word, but it's basically a dirty word in current Western civilization. The post-60s tilt against authority is alive and well. Submission is the key religious word in Islam, where "submission to Allah" is the highest virtue. That stands in stark contrast to modernity and to secularity, where the individual reigns supreme. The poem *Invictus* by William Henley encapsulates the cry of freedom in the enlightenment mind: "I am the master of my fate. I am the captain of my soul." That tells you plainly that submission is out and personal liberation is in.

We get that, I think, as there are so many human authorities not worthy of our allegiance. You wouldn't and shouldn't submit to some frail fool. We are wary of power. We are leery of _obedience_. And yet, the Christ-followers have not signed on to the human declaration of independence.

Christians — like Muslims and most religious people — do not prop humans up as the pinnacle of life. We understand that the Lord God is above us, that He reigns supreme over us puny passing mortals. So, we do believe in submission. We try to hear and obey the voice of Christ. We are called to *"deny ourselves and take up our cross,"* whether we want to or not. We submit. We look to a Higher Power, named the Lord, knowing that we humanoids are deeply flawed.

In Ephesians 5, St. Paul links submission also to marriage. Husband and wife are to *"submit to one another out of reverence to Christ."* To submit means to subject your will and desires for the good of another. Christian love is not a feeling, it's a decision to actively care for and meet the needs of someone else. My job in marriage is to make my wife happy and blessed, (not to aim at making me happy and blessed). How radical is that! It's not only not modern, it's not natural. By nature, life is about numero uno. In Jesus, we believe that His way of service is better and higher. It's heavenly. Sometimes we rise to such heights, by stooping to submit. God has the power to re-orient our wills, from self-service to faith and love. Miraculous, eh. (Or is this too hard to swallow?)

Notes

62
WANT SOME ADVICE FOR BEING A CHRISTIAN?

"Do not be overcome by evil, but overcome evil with good."
— Romans 12:21

You may well want no advice. We humans don't take kindly to it. But, you might be willing to think about your life of faith. As you sit reading this, you know that you are not saved by what you do. A good Lutheran Christian understands that we can never be justified in God's sight by our good works. You know that, right? Never, ever base your security on how well you perform. We are not put right with God by our deeds or merits. Only Jesus saves. His grace is our hope. We are saved *"by grace through faith."* Praise the Lord!

Knowing that, what now? Shall we sit back and relax? Shall we blend in with the world, and drift along the river of life? Well, no. The world is awash in sin and sorrow. The river of life rages, and its current might carry you away. The Christian dares not to complacently flow along merrily down the stream. The worldly waters run to the lowest level, carrying lots of crud and pollution. The Lord has higher ground in mind for us. God wants a people to model His goodness and peace. The Savior not only plucks us from the drowning flow, He also teaches us to navigate the powerful waters. The Good Book is our guide book. Being saved by the goodness of the Lord, there's lots to learn along the way.

If you're open to divine *instructions* for the journey you're on, there's no tighter-packed chunk of the Bible for us Christ-followers than Romans 12. As St. Paul does in most of his letters, after laying out the Gospel to cheer us, he then has a chapter or two of practical instructions to advise us. Romans 12:9-21 has over 30 commands! These include "*hate what is evil*"... "*honor one another*"... "*share with those who are in need*"... "*never flag in zeal*"... "*practice hospitality.*" These pithy imperatives are not a checklist for achieving salvation: no, no, no! They are inspired counsel for life with Christ. Think and pray about each one. I bet that both you and I can find some perfectly relevant items to focus in on. Let them draw you to Jesus and inspire you to heavenly days. In Christ, we can "*overcome evil with good.*" There's a life goal worth shooting for. Biblical teachings can help us answer the question, "What on earth are you doing for heaven's sake?"

Notes

63
WHAT DO PEOPLE PRAY ABOUT?

"To thee, O Lord, I lift up my soul. O my God, in thee I trust."
— Psalm 25:1-2a

Do you ever wonder what your fellow-worshippers are praying about? Each soul who gathers in your sanctuary comes with a lot of life in progress. Some folks may almost skip into church, filled with rich blessings. Others may trudge along the sidewalk, carrying heavy burdens as they come. Each person has their own journey to make, and their own items that occupy their heads and hearts. Both joy and sorrow, both pain and pleasure, are around you in the members of your church family.

Part of the greatness of the Psalms is that they are as diverse as is life. There are Psalms of praise, and of lament. There are Psalms quietly dealing with our inner life, and Psalms soaring joyously into the heavens. The Psalms were the hymnbook of Israel, and though they be now 3,000 years old, yet they speak profoundly the _prayers_ of daily life. If you want help with your personal prayer life, spending time in the Psalms is a real tutorial. I am confident that you will find prayers there that just fit you to a T.

Psalm 25 is the prayer of a faithful person desiring God's aid. It is a humble beseeching of the Lord in the midst of life's challenges. We too come into God's presence trusting He will hear us and help us. Your church family bows their heads and folds their hands in prayer, seeking the intervention of the Almighty into their situations. Be they dealing with illness, entangled in a relational mess, heartsick at some failure or baffled with a difficult decision, they come to the Lord in prayer. Our eternal Friend listens and encourages and responds. What a gift it is, to "take it to the Lord in prayer."

In Psalm 25, the particular requests are for deliverance from enemies (v. 2), guidance in God's will (vs. 4, 5, 8, 9), and forgiveness of sins (v. 7). Don't you suppose that this very day the Christians around you also implore the Lord for deliverance, guidance and mercy? For your need, and for theirs, add your prayers to Him who is our hope and our salvation. The prayers go up and the blessings come down.

Notes

64

ARE CHRISTIANS STRANGE?

"I will bless the Lord at all times; his praise shall continually be in my mouth. My soul makes its boast in the Lord; let the afflicted hear and be glad."
— Psalm 34:1-2

We Christians are not just sorta different. We're like cats and dogs different. A few years back there was a popular book out called *Men are from Mars, Women are from Venus*. You heard of it? It accentuated that our gender difference is like inter-planetary. You might see this, and agree, that cats are not similar to dogs, or that men and women too are worlds apart. Though many things are shared in common, with cats/dogs and with men/women, yet they are far from the same. Yes? So now consider Christians and secularists.

The standard modern Western person is full-tilt into individual autonomy. He/she has a personal agenda, with eyes upon the earth and private pursuits. It's a human-oriented universe: their world revolves around them. Other people can share the stage with them, though most folks are just background props in their personal play. The measuring stick of this earthling success is normally scored in five items: health, wealth, looks, popularity and pleasure. The role-models are celebrities who hit the jackpot on these five markers. It's a material world. The best practitioners of this worldly secular approach dominate. They are the "successes." Plus, they get great media coverage.

The Christian way is alien to that. The Christ-follower lives for a different _purpose_ and marches to a different drummer. Life is not owned by us, nor is about us, nor exists for us. We see the world through different eyes: via a spiritual and eternal lens. We surrender control of the script and are aiming at a different target. We live to glorify the Lord. We are aiming at a much higher horizon than the secularist. Psalm 34 puts it this way: "*I will extol* [that is, "'toll the bell in honor of'"] *the Lord at all times.*" He continues, "*My soul will boast in the Lord; let the afflicted hear and rejoice.*" Hmmm... Even when afflicted, the believer can rejoice? That's not normal, that's not earth-like — that's strange. That's a soul that's been transferred into the Kingdom of Light!

Notes

65

DOES IT MATTER HOW I DRESS?

> *"I will greatly rejoice in the Lord, my soul shall exult in my God; for he has clothed me with the garments of salvation, he has covered me with the robe of righteousness."*
> — Isaiah 61:10a

Far be it from me, a square senior, to pretend to be hip to fashion. I wasn't even a snazzy dresser decades ago, as I've always been more nerdy than natty. Nonetheless, let's ponder our wardrobe a bit today. Isaiah initiates the topic, with his mention of "*garments.*" Most humans care at least somewhat about what they wear. Though most folks are not fashionistas, neither do we want to look unkempt. (There are obviously some folks who work hard at appearing weird and want attention that way, but even those artsy ones don't want to look the part of a dirty bum.) We prefer to have acceptable garments, at a minimum, and probably want to be "dressed for success" among our peers.

There is a salutary Christian aspect to this clothing-talk. Christ-followers know that it's false that "clothes make the man," and we eschew preening and pretense in the wardrobe department. Yet we also can understand the biblical images about how we're dressed. Be it Job: "*I put* on righteousness, and it clothed me; my _justice_ was like a robe and a turban" (Job 29:14); or Paul: "*Put on then, as God's chosen ones, holy and beloved, compassion, kindness, lowliness, meekness and patience*" (Colossians 3:12); or Peter: "*Clothe yourselves, all of you, with humility toward one another*" (1 Peter 5:5); or Jesus Himself: "*I send the promise of my Father upon you; but stay in the city, until you are clothed with power from on high*" (Luke 24:49) — we are addressed as to how we are to be dressed. God cares about our looks. The Lord God has a certain look He wants from us. He is not concerned with our physical attire, but very much wants us clothed with a spirit and a character that befits His family. If we be children of God, we should look the part. It would not reflect well upon the King if His kids move about in the rags of unrighteousness.

To get the suitable attire to properly honor the Master, you don't have to buy it, nor can you earn it, nor can you make-it-yourself. It's a gift! As Isaiah happily announces: "*He has clothed me with the garments of salvation, He has covered me with the robe of righteousness.*" You see the source of the admirable attire? It's all from God. "*He has clothed me.*" To us whose "*righteousness is as filthy rags*" (Isaiah 64:6), He grants the presents that are ours to freely put on. He hands out "*the garments of salvation.*" To be saved is to slip on the peace of mind, purpose of days, joy of life, compassion for fellow-sinners, strength of character, and assurance of heaven that is truly a beautiful look for the mere mortals that we are. God's got us covered. When we put on the goodness of Christ, we are well-dressed indeed.

Notes

66
IS CHRISTIANITY A CAUCASIAN THING?

"Nations shall come to your light, and kings to the brightness of your rising."
— Isaiah 60:3

Some people might think that Christianity is a white folks' religion. Think again. From the day Jesus came, He's been on a global mission. At His birth, magi from the East got an eye-full. They got to see the glory of God revealed in the Babe of Bethlehem. To these kings on camels from across the desert is made known who the Ruler of the universe really is. These are Gentiles, not Jews. They are foreigners, of other tongues, not the chosen people of Abraham. And here they are, in the Nativity story. They were well-off and educated experts in astronomy and ancient writings. (Think: PhD-types). They were Persians, with a wholly different worldview and culture. And yet, here they are, given a key role in the Lord's invasion of Earth. They illustrate the world-wide scope of this Jesus. As the lowly shepherds signify the gift of the Savior for local commoners, now these magi too get a peek at what God has done. These rich and learned foreigners are in on this salvation from on high. Talk about *inclusivity*; the Lord is going all out. Jesus is for everyone! He was multicultural centuries before we knew about that word. He is busting open our little tribal boxes and showing that He is for all people everywhere. It's an epiphany! This was earth-altering! From Jesus' first entry into our human race, it is revealed that God's love is universal.

Now today, can you see how wide is this Child's sway? Isaiah was absolutely correct: "*Nations shall come to your light, and kings to the brightness of your rising.*" Yup, nations and kings across the centuries and around the world do come to Christ's light. Christians come in every color and every language, in all age groups and income levels. Jesus has a global magnetism. Picture it: Jesus is worshipped today in Swahili and in Chinese, and on every continent, and in cathedrals as well as in huts. (FYI: Of the world's six billion people, two billion are Christian; and those Christians are 25% in Europe, 37% in the Americas, 26% in Africa, and 13% in Asia.) Neat, eh? We are the biggest and most diverse movement on Earth! Jesus reigns from pole to pole. We often have a bit of myopia, seeing "Christians" as all just like us, doing worship like we do and fellowshipping in the style we are familiar with. Think bigger, look farther — Jesus is totally global.

Notes

67

WHAT HAPPENS IN BAPTISM?

"We were buried therefore with him by baptism into death, so that as Christ was raised from the dead by the glory of the Father, we too might walk in newness of life."
— Romans 6:4

I know that we normally connect "life" with "good," and "death" with "bad," but let's mess with that for a bit. We who live in relationship with Jesus do a fair amount of turning things upside down, and here we go again. It was He who taught us that "*the last shall be first,*" and "*the servant is the greatest,*" and such. So, we may be somewhat used to this topsy-turvy Master. Ready for a mind-flip regarding baptism?

When you think about *baptism*, your mind goes to what? You think of new life and God's embrace and the washing of regeneration and a beginning in faith and inclusion into the Church and your ordination into the service of Christ, yes? Each of those understandings of baptism are biblical and salutary. We link baptism with life, with hope, with positive blessings coming down.

Our Good Book adds to that a counter-intuitive concept also. The truth from St. Paul as we receive it in Romans 6 is that baptism is also a death. Baptism is deadly. His words in that chapter include "*baptized into His death*" and "*buried with Him through baptism.*" Paul goes on to say that we "*have been united with Him in a death like His,*" and "*our old self was crucified,*" and "*the body ruled by sin might be done away with.*" You see that there is a linkage of baptism and death. You don't want to think of this at the font, especially if you surround a cute and cuddly bambino. Thoughts of death are foreign to such a moment. You are celebrating life and blessings and joy, not anything related to death. Yet the Lord interrupts such a happy occasion by telling us of the death component as well. Baptism marks a death. It connects both with Jesus' death, and with ours.

Baptism is a double-sign. God's action upon the child — or adult — is both a drowning and a raising. Put to death is the dark power of sin and self-centeredness. God drowns our natural bondage to fear and tragedy and brokenness. He breaks the power of Satan. By Jesus' death — attributed now to our account — a victorious killing of evil and hell takes place. Stupendous! We need it! Honest sinners know that we mortals need much more than a religious ritual or a ceremonial initiation or a symbolic reminder of the Almighty's goodwill. We need actual divine rescue! We need liberation from our captivity to sin and despair. This the Savior provides! The deliverance of humanity came directly via the death of Jesus. In holy baptism you get drowned, and you get raised to life forever with God. Thank the Lord: baptism is deadly.

Notes

68
HOW ADAPTABLE CAN WE BE?

"To the weak I became weak, that I might win the weak. I have become all things to all men that I might by all means save some."
— 1 Corinthians 9:22

A person needs to have some flexibility, yes? If one is rigid and never-changing, that's bad, yes? However, to be infinitely malleable, to just change with the wind and do whatever it takes to get elected, like some spineless politicians, that's bad, right? When is adaptability a good thing, and when is it not? St. Paul and the early Christians had lots of discussions (ok, to be accurate, they had arguments) about such matters. The nub of it for them was: how much of the Christian faith was rock-solid and non-negotiable, and how much could be variable? Should they follow most of the older Testament (Jewish) laws, or just drop them? The specific issues in that 1st century were things like circumcision, eating meat that had been offered to idols, polytheism, allegiance to Rome, worshipping on the Sabbath, sexual boundaries, women's roles, etc. Sounds rather dicey eh? _Morality_ always is.

The first Corinthian letter of Paul is heavily about this. It's a series of case studies about church issues and how flexible Christians could or could not be. It's a most intriguing and relevant epistle. In chapter 9, verse 22, we read *"to the weak I became weak, that I might win the weak. I have become all things to all men, that I might by all means save some."* Paul is here championing appropriate flexibility. He would adapt to many local customs if that would advance the Gospel. He would put no unnecessary impediments in the way of Christ's advance. Some opponents of Paul no doubt thought that he was being double-minded. They saw him as weak and fickle, not as helpfully flexible. But there was a method to Paul's malleability. For us today also, consider these two constructs on changeability.

We differentiate between *style* and *substance*. Christian style is very variable. (Think robes vs. casual dress, hymns vs. rock bands, etc.) Christianity can work on Wall Street or on dusty lanes. Christians can witness and serve at either the opera or at NASCAR. In style: be flexible. Yet in substance: be true to Christ. There is a core of Christian truth that does not waver. (We call this orthodox / basic Christianity, as defined by the Creeds and Confessions of the historic Church.)

We understand that some matters are "dogma," some are "doctrine" and some are "adiaphora." Picture these as concentric circles. The central core teachings are "dogma": all Christians hold tight to key tenets. (e.g. The Trinity, the divinity of Christ, the authority of the Bible, etc.). The second ring of the circle is "doctrine": the particular beliefs important to particular branches of the faith (e.g. mode of baptism and communion, view of creation, etc.). Then the outer ring is "adiaphora": external customs and styles (e.g. music type, church governance structure, which holy days, etc.).

We'll keep working on it.

69
ARE CHRISTIANS CRACKPOTS?

"But we have this treasure in earthen vessels, to show that the transcendent power belongs to God and not to us"
— 2 Corinthians 4:7

More than we want to admit: we're broken. I don't just mean the world: "them, out there, those no-good-niks" that we can be outraged about. Rage is all the rage; but is it not the kettle calling the pot black? I'm afraid Pogo was spot-on when he declared: "We have met the enemy, and it is us." One key Christian understanding of life is that fault-finding must start with ourselves. *"First take the log out of your own eye"* is how Jesus put it. Don't you just hate this truth? It's so blasted humbling. No, it's downright humiliating. We are so very imperfect. I hope that we can laugh at ourselves a bit on this, because if not, it is just too depressing. If we will not eat some humble pie as humans, then the choices are either arrogance — if we think that our group is pure and perfect — or despair, if we think that all humans are scumbags.

St. Paul sounds a proper humble note in 2 Corinthians 4. He knows that we Christians have in our hands the glorious treasure of the Gospel, but we fumble it. (Good, good thing that God's promise is unbreakable! Though we botch the handoff, the Gospel remains.) Paul puts it this way: "*what we preach is not ourselves, but Jesus Christ as Lord.*" Paul goes on: "*we have this treasure in earthen vessels.*" These earthen vessels were jars of clay — temporary and fairly fragile pots. We are those mere containers — the short-shelf-life instruments for distributing the real gift. And we are often cracked pots, that leak. Never, ever conflate and confuse Christ with Christians! Don't judge Christ by way of some crackpot. We jars of clay have feet of clay, ya know. Your favorite pastor ever, your shining Gospel singer, your sweet Christian grandma... bless their hearts, but do not expect perfection. Not near. We are but earthen vessels.

    This truth does not demean us; does not mean that we are worthless and useless. Not at all. It does, however, keep our eyes properly fixed on Jesus. It helps us with our _humility_. It keeps us in our place — redeemed sinners — and it keeps Jesus in His: Redeemer of the world.

Notes

70
SHOULD CHRISTIANS BE ACTIVISTS?

"The Lord took me from following the flock, and the Lord said to me 'Go, prophesy to my people Israel.'"
— Amos 7:15

Some Christians think that the Church is cowardly. They say that pastors and churches just keep their heads down and mouths shut in the face of evil. Christian activists believe passionately in social justice and in the Church's role in instigating that. Rather than just safely (and complacently?) being the chaplain to an unjust culture, we need to stand up and speak out.

Such a view is biblical, and right in line with the fiery Amos and the host of Old Testament prophets. If you want your eyebrows singed and your guilt elevated and your outrage activated, read Amos. He was called from being a farmer — working hard and minding his own business, you might say — and became a spokesman to fight for the right. He lambasted the opulent lifestyles and oppressive greed of his nation. He gave them a tongue-lashing for their bribery, immorality and idolatry. He socked it to 'em. Amos and the prophets would not be complacent and shut their eyes to wickedness. They were outspoken activists.

In the Older Testament, God spoke and worked through both prophets and priests. The prophets worked outside the official religious institution, and the priests were the keepers of the institution. Did those two roles conflict, or were they complementary? Did the people need a scolder, or an intercessor? Well... Both. It's rather a "Law and Gospel" thing. Sometimes we need God's correction, and sometimes we need God's mercy. It's rather like good parenting, yes?

When it's time for outrage and agitation... one tip: be careful to line things up right. God gave Amos a "plumb line," a way to judge squarely. The Church's main task is to declare God's mercy in Christ, but when a corrective Word is called for, don't just wing it based on your personal passion or party affiliation. Make sure your prophetic message is aligned with the Word, not some current *political* cause or the spirit of the age.

You might want to get some good wise counsel on such an undertaking.

Notes

71

Is Communion Cannibalism?

"I am the living bread which came down from heaven; if any one eats of this bread, he will live forever; and the bread which I shall give for the life of the world is my flesh."
— John 6:51

Cannibalism? Yikes! Cannibalism is eating human flesh. It has been practiced off and on over the ages, sometimes in emergency desperation, and sometimes in ceremonial ritual. Some cannibals aimed to possess the soul and attributes of the one eaten. Some drank the deceased's blood from skull-cups. Sheesh! To modern sensibilities, this is bizarre and barbaric. The thought of it may be enough to gross you out. With more and more Western refined values, even eating animals is often verbotin, as many diets are now vegetarian and vegan.

Though cannibalism is way, way out in left field, how do Christians think of _communion_ nowadays? Do we keep the language and the imagery of blood, when plenty of well-polished folks would run at the sight of blood? Some branches of the Church avoid any flesh-eating, blood-drinking imagery by understanding communion as symbolic representation. They talk about a "meal of remembrance" or a "table of hospitality." It is presented as inspiring, but scrubbed of any gore. The majority of Christians, however, remain sacramental and don't shy away from the body and blood "real presence" of Christ. So yes, we do believe that we eat and drink Jesus. We don't want just a nice idea about Jesus; we want Him, inside us. We want His life, His Spirit, His soul and attributes, coursing through our veins. We want inner nourishment to refuel us. Just as food must come inside us in order to nourish and fuel our bodies, Jesus does so for our souls. You've heard the expression "you are what you eat"? Uh huh. Spiritual health depends on our ingesting and digesting the Lord. So OK, we are sorta cannibals.

(This is vastly different than the cannibalism of our current political culture, where we kill and eat each other, to our demise. But that's another issue.)

Notes

72
IS CHRISTIANITY EXCLUSIVE?

> *"Now therefore fear the Lord, and serve Him in sincerity and in faithfulness; put away the gods which your fathers served beyond the River, and in Egypt, and serve the Lord."*
> — Joshua 24:14

There are few higher values in our culture than inclusivity. All colleges and workplaces and agencies are downright righteous about being inclusive. To not be inclusive is loudly blamed and shamed. There is proud intolerance of intolerance. Got it. So how on earth can Christians be so closed-minded and exclusive regarding the Lord? We are not fully ecumenical and inter-religious. We definitely do not believe that there are "many paths to God," or that "all roads lead to heaven" or that "all religions are equally good." There are religious people who do believe in those things: they are called Unitarian.

The very first of our 10 Commandments is: *"You shall have no other gods."* (See the full list in Exodus 20.) The Lord is described as *"a jealous God."* Joshua and scads of biblical messages told the people *"throw away the gods of your ancestors, and serve the Lord."* Early Christians were put to death because they proclaimed *"Jesus is Lord"* and

– 148 –

they would bow to no other. We will not demote Jesus to just one member of the world's pantheon. So, obviously, this is trouble. This is not politically correct. This is not fully *inclusive*. Is it more accurate to say that this is an "inclusive exclusivity"? That is: all are welcome and invited (inclusive), but invited only to the Lord (exclusive).

Many people do not believe in objective truth these days. Many are "post-modern" (in that people get to decide their own truth). But does not reality tell us that some things are true and real and not subject to our manipulation? (Gravity is true whether you want to believe it or not, for example.) We humans just don't get to decide everything. One of those things is who God is. If there is a God, He decides who He is, right? The Lord made us in His image, and evidently some folks now want to return the favor. Nice try.

Notes

73
DO I HAVE TO TELL OTHERS ABOUT JESUS?

"Go therefore and make disciples of all nations"
— Matthew 28:19

Lots of folks recoil from "have to's." It's a rather natural resistance. We do not like being told we "have to." Right? Now, add to it that Protestant Christianity was birthed in opposition to "have to's." Luther and the reformers realized we can't meet all of God's commands and we can never be put right with Him via "have to's." The whole Law vs. Gospel dynamic of our faith teaches us that the Law — "have to's" / "shoulds" — says "do," while the Gospel says "done." We rejoice that we are not saved by what we do, but by what the Lord has done. Got it. Love it. So, any "have to's" are not tied to our salvation. God loves you, period. That's grace. So, you don't "have to" tell others about Jesus to be saved. (A sigh of relief goes up from many a Christian.)

With that theological hurdle out of the way, now... a second hurdle is psychological. Some would say you shouldn't even ask such a question. That is, a true believer doesn't "have to" tell others, she "wants to." You see the

– 150 –

difference? Some say a genuine faith naturally produces lips that speak up for Jesus. To ask "do I have to?" — like "do I have to kiss my wife?" — shows a bad heart. It reveals a deeper problem. They'd say that the question itself is faulty. They'd say that Christians just naturally want to tell others, and they don't need to be told to do it. I used to think that.

We humans, being the gnarly weaklings that we are, need help — we need a push. So, "Yes," you have to <u>witness</u> to others. We are commanded to get the Word out. Our deeds alone are just not exemplary enough. If you want others to know Jesus, and want His kingdom of love to spread, words are required. St. Paul wrote: *"How are people to call upon Him in whom they have not believed? And how are they to believe in Him of whom they have never heard?"* (Romans 10:14). They have to hear the words, not just guess at our motivations. If you're OK with people living and dying outside the faith of Jesus — outside His sweet blessings — you don't "have to." If you want Him to win and darkness to lose — find a way. You don't have to yell it out at the corner, but think of ways to tell the Good News. It's our job. You can do it: be a warm, winsome witness.

Notes

74
ARE YOU READY FOR THE WORST?

"Beloved, do not be surprised at the fiery ordeal which comes upon you to prove you, as though something strange were happening to you."
— 1 Peter 4:12

Have you heard of "preppers"? These are folks who are taking disaster preparedness seriously. They are making plans. A guy in the Twin Cities has a detailed plan.

1. He owns wooded property up north.
2. He built a "tiny house" on wheels that is equipped and ready to go.
3. He has a 1972 pickup to pull it.

Why 1972? That's before our autos had a computer system, so that it would start and run even after an EMP blast. Were there a nuclear bomb with Electro-Magnetic Pulse, it would knock out the power grid. Thus: no computers, no electricity, no gas pumps, etc. The world as we know it would crawl and brawl in the face of such an apocalyptic disaster. It'd be "doomsday" of sorts.

Now, please don't panic. Such a scenario seems highly unlikely, (except in a Hollywood script). Go on about your business. However... the rational earthling does know that bad days are coming. They come. Whether suddenly via accident or stroke or war or market crash, or perhaps slowly via age — the _end of the world_ comes for each of us. No one gets out unscathed and alive. Don't dwell on that and let it make you morbid and crazy, but be prepared.

The Bible has many admonitions to "*make the most of the time, because the days are evil*" (Ephesians 5:16). We don't want to be caught off-guard when the day comes "*like a thief in the night*" (Luke 12:39). To be a Christian prepper, be well-fed with the Bread of Life, filled up with Jesus' Living Water, armed with the Weapons of the Spirit, and invested in Treasure in Heaven. Have those spiritual resources stored up. Be on good speaking terms with your Creator, and surrounded by your company of saints. You'll make it. Whatever manner of "the worst" befalls you, when the curtain drops, you'll be covered. We don't predict that Day, or go bonkers in fear about it, but we are mindful of our passing days, and we know that on the other side of our exit door the Lord has the welcome mat out and ready for us. Carry on.

Notes

75

IS CHRISTIANITY CONSERVATIVE OR LIBERAL?

> *"But he, desiring to justify himself, said to Jesus, 'and who is my neighbor?'"*
> — Luke 10:29

What an easy question. Of course, it's both. Just don't try to tell that to someone who is passionately partisan. They will tell you — or yell you — in no uncertain terms that "conservative Christian" is an oxymoron. Or vice versa, depending on which gang they're in. Just to utter their opposing word — "conservative" or "liberal" — is a fighting word. (Fighting as in mud-wrestling, quite often.) For a good percentage of Americans, <u>politics</u> is the new religion. That is, the passion and fervor and highest value of their heart revolves around their political party. There's more jumping and shouting at a campaign rally or a protest than at church.

Both red and blue teams want to capture the Christians for their purposes. Since "Jesus is Lord" for us, any political allegiance is secondary. Fact: many Christians are conservative. Fact: many Christians are liberal. Christians want to love their neighbors, and politics is one avenue for doing that, but there are different ways to do it. If "every good why needs a good how," the Christ-followers know why politics matter but don't agree on how. How to best love your neighbor is debatable. (Though the verse above, as the lead-in to the Good Samaritan parable, makes it clear that loving your neighbor does take concrete action.)

A conservative wants to conserve what is good, appreciates traditional values, and prioritizes things like safety, responsibility and fiscal restraint. A liberal wants to liberate people from oppression, appreciates new visions and prioritizes good government programs. None of those are anti-Christian. All of those can fit with good biblical themes. Each political party says that they are promoting hope and peace and liberty and neighborly love. No doubt there are good and smart folks on each team.

Not to quench your vigor in the public arena, but "*put not your trust in princes*" (Psalm 146). To use biblical government categories: neither Pharaoh nor Caesar nor zealots can save us. Human institutions are never Messianic. Don't get sucked into that, or you will hate a lot of people. Do your best with politics and do your duty to citizenship — but keep it secondary. Christians have only one King.

(If this sounds just too dispassionate... I am out of my element. And mud-wrestling is just not for me.)

Notes

76
IS IT OK TO BE RICH?

> *"For it is easier for a camel to go through the eye of a needle than for a rich man to enter the kingdom of God."*
> — Luke 18:25

As we know, some people are rich and some are not. As some wag put it: "Half the world is dieting, and the other half is starving." Some folks callously think this situation is just fine; it's just the way the cookie crumbles. Perhaps they even think those who are rich have earned it and deserve it; and likewise that those who are poor have caused their poverty. (An honest researcher could find examples of those whose actions triggered their situation, as well as those whose didn't.)

Whatever the root causes for riches and poverty, the Christ-followers aim to respond with:

1. Humility, and
2. Generosity.

Christians who are more politically oriented would want to add...

3. Advocacy.

The goodness of God and the gifts of skills or smarts, as well as a prosperous nation and a bountiful creation, all contribute to riches. Arrogance about wealth is a foolish response. (And keep in mind: "No matter how big your house, you go out in a box.") Children of God know that all good things are gifts from the Father's hand. Therefore, we are grateful, and we want to be generous, as the Lord is. The riches are not ours, but belong to the Lord, for us to share. Please don't kid yourself: most Americans are among the richest people in the world. So, share. No stinginess nor hoarding is allowed. Rather, we are to tithe. (That is, give away at least 10% as the Bible teaches us.)

Having said these basics, the question remains: is it OK to be rich? Many godly people in the Bible were rich, so we don't equate riches with wickedness. But Jesus often talked about the danger of wealth, and how it can impede love and faith. He said, "*...where your treasure is, there will your heart be also*" (Matthew 6:21). He said, "*You cannot serve God and money*" (Matthew 6:24). It perhaps is OK to be rich, but you're on thin ice, eh?

Notes

77
ARE CHRISTIANS BETTER THAN NON-CHRISTIANS?

"All have sinned and fall short of the glory of God."
— Romans 3:23

A person might figure that Christians should be a cut above. After all, we've got the 10 Commandments and our fellow-believer support team, we're privy to Jesus' teachings and we've been given the Holy Spirit. We should be better, right? We kinda have the "home-field advantage" with Jesus. Nevertheless, I'm sorry to tell you that we often aren't better. We stumble and bumble like everybody else. Our flaws and sins are ample. Even the finest Christians are imperfect. This disappointing reality is why some in the world think that we church-folk are "hypocrites." Now, if we claimed to be superior, we'd earn that "H"-label. Indeed, an arrogant Christian would be worse, not better, than non-Christians. (Hollywood often loves this eventuality.)

If we understand our faith correctly, we know that we're not perfect, just forgiven. We aren't better than anyone else. Yet with God's grace we can be better than we used to be. The Lord can develop us into instruments that are useful to

Him. Take a little hope in that today. Don't compare yourself to others — Christians or not — just be glad that God is at work.

When you get disappointed by Christians — or even by yourself — try to practice your _humility_. God isn't finished with you, or others, yet. We're "under construction." Perhaps you've heard the expression: "Church isn't a museum for saints but a hospital for sinners." A hospital is where folks go to get well. They are there 'cuz they're not well. Jesus said, "*Those who are well have no need of a physician, but those who are sick. I came not to call the righteous, but sinners*" (Matthew 9:12). I suppose it'd make sense that you'd find healthier people at a museum than at a hospital. That's not to say that church people are sicker... but it might increase your compassion for other Christians if you know we're all sinners in need of grace. We're not in church pretending to be superior; we're there praying for the Lord to heal and strengthen us. Don't be surprised by human failings; be grateful that the good Lord is patient. His lovingkindness endures forever.

Notes

78
MUST I CHOOSE BETWEEN SECULAR VALUES AND CHRISTIAN VALUES?

"For though we live in the world we are not carrying on a worldy war."
— 2 Corinthians 10:3

More people are able to use an axe than a scalpel. It is easier and quicker to swing the axe than to cut with the care and precision of the scalpel. Lots of folks aren't able to (or don't want to) cut carefully concerning secular and Christian. Hasty talkers on each side would blurt that, "Yes, you must choose." They see a sharp binary choice between the world's views and the Church's views. Their battle lines are drawn and the fight is on for them. Their paradigm is science vs. religion, evolution vs. creation, reason vs. faith, church vs. state, conservative vs. liberal, etc. It's "either / or" for them.

A reasonable believer recognizes that we have lots of values in common with unbelievers. Such as? They love peace and justice, so do we. They oppose oppression and poverty, so do we. I'd go so far as to say that we did so first. The secular West is founded in Christian values. Things like global concern, individual rights, compassion, charity, servant leadership, democracy, etc., all developed out of

Christianity. Today, some secularists want the fruit but not the tree. They may hack at the roots and not want Jesus, but they approve much of Jesus' teachings from which Western civilization grew. Thus, do affirm those mutual values when you can. Work together on good things.

I do realize there is lots of clashing too. There is some "culture war" underway. Battle lines do exist regarding sexual behaviors, religious freedom, sanctity of life, materialism and self-esteem, for instance. There are clear differences between a secular *worldview* and a Christian worldview. We can't just go along to get along. Sometimes, as James wrote: "*...friendship with the world is enmity with God*" (James 4:4). Christians do not hate the world and oppose all its views and values. Clearly not. But we stand strong and distinct as needed. "*We must obey God rather than men*" (Acts 5:29). Our true, time-tested values that serve as our plumb-line are drawn from the Word of God. So marinate in the Word, and work on applications with other faith-folk. It's no snap, but it is vital.

Notes

79
WHO SHOULD I GIVE TO?

> *"God is able to provide you with every blessing in abundance, so that you may always have enough of everything and may provide in abundance for every good work."*
> — 2 Corinthians 9:8

I'd guess that many of you have daily mail similar to mine. The mail carrier brings me a personal card or letter rarely, a bill to pay a couple times a week, a mass mailing advertisement every day or so, and three or four requests for *money* every day. Every day those solicitations for my financial aid arrive. The appeals come from various NGOs, from schools and hospitals and camps, from political causes, from Christian ministries, etc. I am asked to save the whales, to support missionaries, to feed the hungry, to fund scholarships, to fight diseases, etc. I get asked. You likely do also.

We Christ-followers are taught to give. Generosity is part of the deal for us Christians. Unless tithing is one of those biblical teachings that you have deemed no longer binding, we have our orders. We are to give 10%, and to do less is robbery. (See Malachi 3:8.) We are blessed so that we can also bless. We are to give regularly, proportionately and cheerfully.

— 162 —

If you have your mind aligned with this principle and your heart warmed to share as the Lord intends, then you are most of the way there. Many Christians just can't get themselves to be sacrificially generous. They maybe would like to, and they think it's a nice idea, but difficulty of circumstance and / or lack of willpower work to sabotage their good intentions. For those who have answered, "Why should I give?" and "How can I pull it off," the third question is, "Who should I give to?"

This is where the fun begins. It is a rewarding delight to be able to give. It is a joy to have the freedom to direct finances to forward the love of God and the love of neighbor. There are so very many excellent ways to bless humanity via your contribution. Who is it that needs your help? What causes move your heart? Some givers like to focus on just a few charities, to make a bigger impact. Others like to spread their giving around and support lots of organizations. Some give to a wide variety of causes, both Christian and secular. Others hone in on groups that are overtly Christian, so that the Name of Jesus is always part of what is given. However you do your discerning, check out the recipients to see if they steward the money well. (Sad to say, there are some charlatans out there who take too big a chunk of your donation for administration.) The main thing is: do it. And have fun. It's a privilege to give.

(PS: My wife and I have chosen The Salvation Army, Lutheran World Relief, Habitat for Humanity Prison Fellowship, and Union Gospel Mission as among our main recipients. There are good choices galore.)

Notes

80
SHOULD WE PRAISE GOD IN OUR TROUBLES?

"Give thanks in all circumstances; for this is the will of God in Christ Jesus for you."
— 1 Thessalonians 5:18

Phoney baloney. That's what most earthlings would call praising God when you are hurting. Our very natural and heartfelt response when things are going bad is feeling bad. When your troubles have mounted up, the reaction is lament. We groan or cry or shake our heads or scream or sit in glum silence. When life hurts, we hurt. That is our normal and even healthy response. We should pour out our hearts to the Lord; and His shoulders are plenty big enough for us to cry on. It's ok. Let it out. (The Psalms are filled with laments.)

Sometimes an additional response can be added to that sorrow. Sometimes we are granted the gift of <u>*praise*</u> even right in the dark valley. Strange as this may sound, maybe you'll consider it. Have you heard this poem: "When the night is darkest, the stars shine brightest"? The purity and greatness of the Lord might be clearest to us in contrast to the tribulations of earth. When we are in the midst of great loss or failure.... awash in the setbacks and sorrows of this wounded world....face-to-face with the depravity of man and the ravages of nature and the futile, fleeting vanity of life.... Oh, how glorious is the eternal, invincible and finally victorious Lord of heaven and earth! Praise be to the Immortal One who is enthroned above our mortal muck!

Praise for the Lord at a time when my personal life is in the dumper clearly means that the praise is not focused on nor dependent on me. That's a radical concept in an age that is very self-centric. It declares that God's praise is not contingent on my personal circumstances or feelings. I need not veto the honor the Almighty is due because I am having a bad day. I can celebrate God's goodness even when I am not the recipient of it (in ways that I notice). I may be sick, but others are healthy: Praise the Lord. I may have a messy family, but others are united: Praise the Lord. I may feel badly, but God is still God. He is still good, still reigning today, and will prevail in paradise.

Praise comes easily when all is well and life is easy. We sing "when we're happy and we know it, praise the Lord". It can also come when troubles are huge, because the contrast between our dark days and God's eternal radiance is so vivid. Knowing that Christ was crucified, yet now reigns, and has won a seat for us at the heavenly party, is the praise that overcomes the world.

His star shines brightest on the darkest of nights.

Notes

Topical Index

Keyword...Devotion   Check These Verses

Baptism...67   Acts 2:38; Romans 6:4; Titus 3:4-7
Calling from God...41   1 Samuel 3:1-11; Isaiah 6:1-8; Acts 9:1-10
Church...53, 57, 77   Acts 2:42-47; Hebrews 10:23-25;
    1 Peter 2:9-10
Communion...71   Matthew 26:26-28; John 6:47-51;
    1 Corintians 11:23-26
Conversion...55   Matthew 4:18-20; Galatians 1:13-24;
    1 Timothy 2:1-6
Death/Mortality...9, 13, 50   Romans 14:7-9; Philippians 1:21-26;
    1 Thessalonians 4:13-14
Disagreement...6, 7, 70   Ezekiel 3:16-18; Amos 5:14-15;
    Luke 4:18-19
Doubt/Discouragement...1, 2, 9, 20, 33   Psalm 14:2-5;
    Ecclesiastes 1:12-18; Galatians 6:9
End of the World...74   Matthew 24; Luke 12:35-40; 1 Peter 4:7
Enemies...25   Psalm 3, 59:1-4; Matthew 5:43-48
Evidence for God/Hidden God...32, 39, 43, 49   Isaiah 40:15-28;
    Psalm 19:1-4; Romans 1:19-23
Faith/Trust...18, 34, 36, 56, 58   Psalm 23; Hebrews 11;
    1 John 4:13-16
Fears...22   John 14:27; Romans 8:31-39; 1 John 4:16-19
Forgiveness...8   Genesis 50:15-21; Matthew 18:21-22;
    Ephesians 4:21-22
God's Discipline...47   Jeremiah 23:1-3; Hosea 6:1-5;
    Hebrews 12:5-13
God's Laws/Instructions...5, 31, 62   Leviticus 19:1-18;
    Psalm 19:7-14; Matthew 7:12
God's Love...30, 34   John 3:16-17; Romans 5:6-8; 1 John 4:7-16
God's Sovereignty...46, 48   Jonah 1:1-4; Matthew 23:37;
    Mark 6:1-5
Holy Spirit...44, 53   John 14:16-17; 1 Corinthians 12:1-7;
    Ephesians 1:11-14

Humility...11, 69, 77   Philippians 2:1-4; 1 Corinthians 1:26-31;
   2 Corinthians 4:5-7
Inclusivity/Unity...4, 66, 72   Isaiah 60:1-3; Acts 10:34-36;
   Revelation 14:6-7
Jesus...38, 39, 40   John 1:1-14; Colossians 1:13-20;
   Hebrews 1:1-4
Justice/Morality...12, 21, 35, 65, 68   Psalm 37:28; Micah 6:8;
   Colossians 3:12-15
Kingdom of God...42   Matthew 9:35-38; Mark 1:14-15;
   Luke 4:18-19
Money/Prosperity...19, 76, 79   Matthew 6:19-24; Luke 18:18-27;
   1 John 3:17-18
Obedience...15, 61   Proverbs 3:5-6; John 14:15; James 4:7
Parenting...15, 26   Psalm 127:3-5; Luke 2:51-52; Ephesians 6:1-4
Peace...22, 60   John 14:27; Ephesians 2:13-18; 1 Peter 3:10-11
Perfection (not!)...59, 69, 77   Job 15:14-16; Romans 3:10,23;
   Ephesians 2:8-9
Politics...70, 75   Psalm 146:3; Jeremiah 29:7; 1 Peter 2:13-17
Prayer...63   Psalm 25:1-2; Matthew 7:7-11; Philippians 4:6
Providence...17, 34, 49   Isaiah 55:10-11; Matthew 6:25-26;
   Ephesians 3:20-21
Purpose/Goals...10, 64   Acts 26:16-18; Ephesians 1:3-10;
   Philippians 3:14
Satan...51   Matthew 4:1-11; James 4:7; 1 Peter 5:8
Spiritual...16, 27   Acts 17:22-23; 1 Corintians 2:12-14;
   2 Corinthians 4:16-18
Trinity...29, 45   Matthew 28:19; Matthew 3:16-17; Acts 2:32-33
Truth...3   Jeremiah 23:28-32; John 8:31-32; 2 Corinthians 4:1-2
Wisdom...14, 24   Psalm 19:7; Proverbs 1:1-9; James 3:17
Witness...73   Matthew 4:18-19; Romans 10:14-15;
   2 Timothy 4:2-5
Worldview...23, 64, 78   John 17:14-18; 2 Corinthians 10:3-5;
   James 4:4
Worship/Praise...36, 54, 56, 80   Psalm 96; Philippians 4:4-9;
   Col 3:15-17

About the Author

Chris Brekke leads a double life: going back and forth between Minnesota and Wisconsin where his two sons and families live. Don't say that he's bi-polar, but, in a geographical way, he is. He also has no current occupation, but keeps himself occupied. Chris was a Lutheran pastor for 38 years, serving in Nebraska, Colorado and Minnesota.

You may contact him at:
pcbrekmn@gmail.com

Other books by Chris Brekke:

Faith Appetizers (2008)

Joke Devotions (2012)

One by One (2012)

Joke Devotions 2 (2015)

Ambidextrous Christianity (2017)

Available from Chris at:
pcbrekmn@gmail.com

or from Sola Publishing at:
solapublishing.com